BERLITZ®

DISCOVER
CALIFORNIA

Edited and Designed by
D & N Publishing,
Lambourn, Berkshire.

All cartography by Hardlines, Charlbury, Oxfordshire, except maps on pages 96, 217, 265, by Visual Image, Street, Somerset.

Photographic Acknowledgements

Front cover: the Lone Cypress, Pebble Beach, by Craig Cary, PhD.

Back cover: San Francisco; reproduced courtesy of the San Francisco Convention and Visitor's Bureau.

All photographs in this book were specially taken or supplied by a variety of individuals and organisations, all of whom are credited in the column opposite.

Although we have made every effort to ensure the accuracy of all the information in this book, changes occur incessantly. We cannot therefore take responsibility for facts, addresses and circumstances in general that are constantly subject to alteration.

 The Berlitz tick is used to indicate places or events of particular interest.

Phototypeset by Wyvern Typesetting Ltd., Bristol.

Printed by C.S. Graphics, Singapore.

Acknowledgements

The author extends her sincere appreciation to the following organizations for their help and cooperation in the research for this book: Anaheim Area Visitors' and Convention Bureau; Avis Rent-A-Car; British Airways; California Deserts Tourism Association; California Office of Tourism; El Dorado County Chamber of Commerce; Eureka/Humboldt County Convention and Visitors' Bureau; Greater Los Angeles Visitors' and Convention Bureau; Hearst Monument; J. Paul Getty Museum; Lake Tahoe Visitors' Authority; Merced Convention and Visitors' Bureau; Modesto Convention and Visitors' Bureau; Monterey Peninsula Visitors' and Convention Bureau; Napa Valley Conference and Visitors' Bureau; Northwest Airlines; Palm Springs Desert Resorts Convention and Visitors' Bureau; Paramount Pictures Corporation; Redwood Empire Association; Sacramento Convention and Visitors' Bureau; San Diego Convention and Visitors' Bureau; San Francisco Convention and Visitors' Bureau; San Luis Obispo County Visitors' and Conference Bureau; Santa Barbara Conference and Visitors' Bureau; Sequoia Kings Canyon National Parks Guest Services; Shasta Cascade Wonderland Association; Sonoma County Convention and Visitors' Bureau; Tahoe North Visitors' and Convention Bureau; Yosemite Park and Curry Co.

Great thanks must also go to these individuals who helped make the work on this book such a pleasure:

Carol Levin, Fred Sater, Betsy Parisoli, Katie Meyer, my patient and invaluable travel companions, Renee and George, my brother Craig, and my husband, Guy.

If you have any new information, suggestions or corrections to contribute to this guide, we would like to hear from you. Please write to Berlitz Publishing at the above address.

BERLITZ®

DISCOVER
CALIFORNIA

Pam Cary

Contents

CALIFORNIA: FACTS AND FIGURES 7

Travelling to California 7
Passports and Visas 9
Customs and Regulations 10
Currency, Travellers' Cheques
   and Credit Cards 10
Weights, Measures and Sizes 10
Travel Insurance 10
Electrical Appliances 11
Travelling within California 14
Language 15
Drinking 15
Communication Services 15
Emergencies 15
Holidays 16
Shopping 16
Tipping 16
National and State Parks 16
Climate 17

THE STATE, ITS HISTORY AND ITS PEOPLE 19

History 19
Geography and Geology 25
Climate 29
Nationalities and Politics 31
The People, Culture
   and Lifestyles 33
FESTIVALS AND EVENTS 36

ON THE SHORTLIST 40

LEISURE ROUTES AND THEMES 43

SAN DIEGO COUNTY 59

ORANGE COUNTY AND THE INLAND EMPIRE 83

DISNEYLAND 98

GREATER LOS ANGELES 111

THE DESERTS 157

DEATH VALLEY NATIONAL MONUMENT 167

THE CENTRAL COAST 173

THE CENTRAL VALLEY 211

THE GOLD COUNTRY 229

THE HIGH SIERRA 241

YOSEMITE NATIONAL PARK 249

SAN FRANCISCO BAY AREA 261

THE NORTH COAST 287

WINE TASTING IN THE NAPA AND SONOMA VALLEYS 290

SHASTA CASCADE 307

USEFUL ADDRESSES AND INFORMATION 314

HOTELS AND RESTAURANTS 321

Index 329

Everything You Need to Know Before Departure

It is always a good idea before departing on a long-distance trip, which getting to California might be, to be as prepared and organized as possible. You will get so much more out of your holiday if you make yourself as familiar with your destination as you can before your arrival. Here is the basic information you will need.

Travelling to California

Before departing for California, contact the United States Tour and Travel Administration (USTTA) in your country. They are an invaluable resource for any traveller, providing information, advice and facts wherever your chosen destination may be.

Yosemite Falls, which with a total drop of 730 m (2,400 ft) is the tallest waterfall in Yosemite National Park, plunges in two sections and is one of the main attractions in the valley.

By Air
If travelling to California, here are the main international airports within the state, depending on your destination:

San Diego International Airport (Lindbergh Field)
3707 N. Harbor Drive
San Diego 92101. Tel. (619) 231-5220.
Located just 5 km (3 miles) northwest of downtown San Diego and a convenient alternative for Los Angeles. Served by major international, national and commuter airlines, airport transport and major car hire agencies.

Los Angeles International Airport (LAX)
1, World Way, Los Angeles, 90009
Tel. (213) 646-4267.

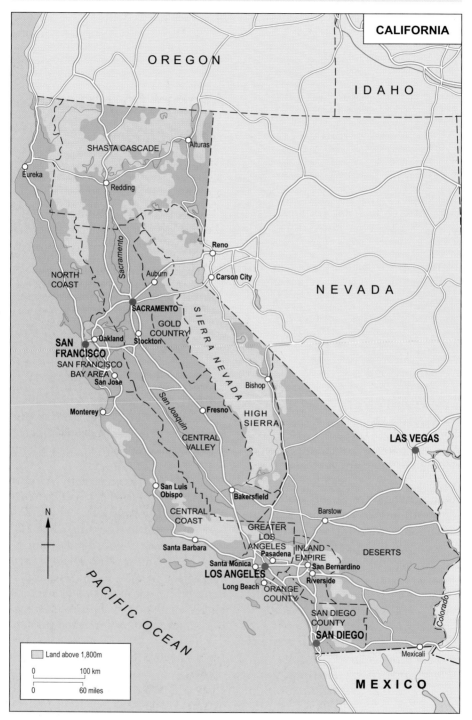

This, the largest airport in southern California, is located on the west side of the city, approximately 45 minutes from Anaheim, and is served by all major international, national and commuter airlines, airport transport and major car hire agencies. For easy access to greater Los Angeles, Orange County and San Diego.

Ontario International Airport (ONT) Ontario, 91761. Tel. (714) 983-8282.
Located approximately 45 minutes from the Anaheim area. Served by international, national, and commuter airlines, airport transport and major car hire agencies. For easy access to Orange County and Los Angeles.

Metropolitan Oakland International (OAK)
530, Waters Street
Oakland, 94607. Tel. (415) 577-4000.
Across the Bay. Served by international, national and commuter airlines, airport transport and major car hire agencies. For easy access to Oakland, Sonoma, Napa Valley and the San Francisco Bay area.

San Francisco International (SFO) Interstate 101. Tel. (415) 761-0800).
Located 23 km (14 miles) south of downtown San Francisco and the eighth largest airport in the country. Served by international, national and commuter airlines, airport transport and major car hire agencies. For easy access to Oakland, San Francisco and San Mateo.

*T*he main cities, towns and roads of California.

International Airlines

The following selection of international airlines operate direct flights from Europe to California. The addresses and telephone numbers are those of the airline headquarters.

American Airlines
PO Box 619616
DFW International Airport
Texas 75261-9616, USA
Tel. (817) 963-1234.

British Airways
PO Box 10, Heathrow Airport
London TW6 2JA, England
Tel. (081) 759-5511.

United Airlines Inc. (UA)
PO Box 66100
O'Hare International Airport,
Chicago, ILL. 60666, USA
Tel. (312) 952-4000.

Virgin Atlantic Airways Ltd
Sussex House, High Street, Crawley
Sussex RH10 1DQ, England
Tel. (0293) 562345.

Time Difference

California is in the Pacific Time Zone (Greenwich Mean Time minus eight hours).

Passports and Visas

Visitors to the United States must have a passport and visa, except for Canadian citizens or British citizens travelling on business, or visitors staying no longer than 90 days and with a return ticket. Contact your nearest United States Embassy or Consulate for all current visitor visa, passport and health requirements necessary to enter the United States.

Customs Regulations

All non-residents entering California must complete customs and immigration formalities at the first point of arrival in the United States, that is even though such a point may be only an intermediate stop *en route*. All items brought into the country must be declared on a form filled in before you arrive and presented at the US Customs on arrival. Prohibited items are listed on the declaration form. Restricted goods include: firearms and ammunition, agricultural products (no fresh meat, fruit or plants), endangered species or their by-products, narcotics, toxic substances and obscene articles or publications. Nonresident visitors to California are allowed to bring in duty free: 200 cigarettes or 1.4 kg (3 lbs) of tobacco; 50 cigars; and 0.946 litres (1.7 pints) of spirits or wine; and up to $100 worth of gifts. Although there is no limit on the amount of US or foreign currency brought into the States, money in excess of $10,000 must be reported to the US Customs.

Currency, Traveller's Cheques and Credit Cards

One dollar is equal to 100 cents. Coins are: 1c (a penny); 5c (a nickel); 10c (a dime); 25c (a quarter). Notes are: $1; $5; $10; $20; $50; $100. Visitors can exchange foreign currency at many, but not all, banks and independent currency exchange bureaux during normal banking hours (9 a.m.–3 p.m., Monday to Friday). However, traveller's cheques in US dollars are by far the most convenient as they are accepted in most shops, hotels and restaurants and can be replaced if lost or stolen. International airports, such as Los Angeles and San Francisco, have currency exchange offices in the international arrival halls, with extended operation hours to suit incoming flights. As the exchange rate fluctuates constantly, it is best to check the current rate of exchange at banks and foreign exchange agencies. Major credit cards, such as Visa, Master Charge and American Express, are accepted in most restaurants and hotels. Visa and Master Charge are usually accepted in shops and petrol stations.

Weights, Measures and Sizes

The Americans have, as yet, no intention of moving over to the metric system. There are, however, some exceptions to their steadfast maintenance of imperial measurements (wine and spirits are purchased in litre bottles and food products are often marked in ounces and grammes).

Travel Insurance

As there is no compulsory or government health plan in the United States, visitors are advised to purchase travel and health insurance to cover them in an emergency (see EMERGENCIES).

Electrical Appliances

If you are travelling with any electrical appliances, such as hair drier or irons, you may need a transformer (240–110V) and an adaptor plug as 110 volts (60 cycles) is standard throughout the US. Transformers are best purchased before leaving home though converter kits can be purchased in the United States from electrical shops. US electrical sockets use plugs with two flat pins lying parallel with an upper round earth pin for earthed electrical items such as an iron.

Travelling within California

By Air

Travelling by air within California is convenient and relatively inexpensive and is certainly a quick way to cover a lot of territory. Internal airports are dotted all around the state and you may be very surprised where you can actually fly into. For information on local flights, airlines and reservations, call (0800) 555-1212, or check in the Yellow Pages.

The following selection of airlines fly within California.
United Airlines: Tel. (312) 952-4000.
US Air: Tel. (202) 783-4500.
Trans World Airlines (TWA):
  Tel. (914) 242-3000.
Pacific Coast Airlines:
  Tel. (714) 833-1955.
Delta Airlines: Tel. (404) 765-2600.
Continental Airlines:
  Tel. (713) 630-5000.
American Airlines:
  Tel. (817) 963-1234.
Northwest Airlines:
  Tel. (612) 726-2111.

By Train

AMTRAK (America's national railroad passenger corporation) serves 72 cities and towns throughout California, and offers a variety of tours throughout the state. Bargain fares and special

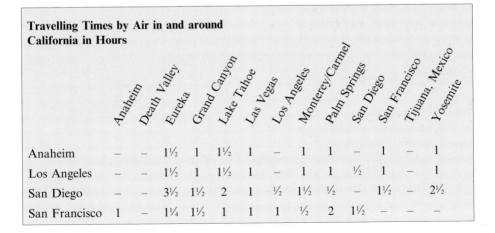

Travelling Times by Air in and around California in Hours

	Anaheim	Death Valley	Eureka	Grand Canyon	Lake Tahoe	Las Vegas	Los Angeles	Monterey/Carmel	Palm Springs	San Diego	San Francisco	Tijuana, Mexico	Yosemite
Anaheim	–	–	1½	1	1½	1	–	1	1	–	1	–	1
Los Angeles	–	–	1½	1	1½	1	–	1	1	½	1	–	1
San Diego	–	–	3½	1½	2	1	½	1½	½	–	1½	–	2½
San Francisco	1	–	1¼	1½	1	1	1	½	2	1½	–	–	–

A taste of rail travel during the history of America can be had at the California State Railroad Museum, Sacramento.

family and excursion rates are often on offer, and a USA Railpass or Far Western Region Rail Passes can be purchased from abroad. To make reservations within California, contact: Show Train Inc., 25, Maiden Lane, Suite 650, San Francisco, 94108.Tel. (415) 362-1439—local; (0800) 227-4248—toll free USA and Canada.

By Bus
Trailways and Greyhound Lines are the two main bus companies offering transportation throughout the state (and the United States). By purchasing a ticket from one destination to another, you are allowed to make as many stops as you like before the

ticket expiry date. Compare first the cost of bus travel and air travel—the bus may not be cheaper. Call information (0800) 555-1212 or look in the phone book for reservations.

For local bus transportation, most areas are served very well by regional bus companies. Details can be obtained from the tourist office or check in the Yellow Pages.

Car Rental
Renting a car is generally very simple but do look around as costs and deals vary. If you are expecting to cover quite a distance, companies that offer a flat rate with unlimited mileage are your best bet. (For individual companies at main destinations *see* pages 315–19.) If arriving by aeroplane, hiring a car at the airport is very straightforward. You will need a credit card to use as a deposit, and an up-to-date driving licence or International Driving Permit. Most car rental companies require the driver to be over 21.

Driving Times in and around California in Hours

	Anaheim	Death Valley	Eureka	Grand Canyon	Lake Tahoe	Las Vegas	Los Angeles	Monterey/Carmel	Palm Springs	San Diego	San Francisco	Tijuana, Mexico	Yosemite
Anaheim	–	5½	14	10	9	5	1	5½	1½	1½	8½	2½	6½
Los Angeles	1	4½	13	7	8	5½	–	4½	2½	2½	7½	3	6
San Diego	1½	8	15½	7½	11½	7½	2½	7½	3	–	10	½	8½
San Francisco	8½	11½	6	16½	4	12	7½	2½	10	10	–	10½	4

The American Automobile Association (AAA)

If you are planning to drive long or short distances through California, be sure to contact or preferably visit the nearest American Automobile Association office. They are most helpful and can provide you with directions and maps for wherever you are planning to go, and advice if you are not so sure. You can also take out short-term insurance here.

Driving

Throughout the United States, driving is on the right. Travelling by car in California is a way of life and the road system is excellent, although be prepared to hit a lot of traffic in some of the major cities. Travelling on the freeways and highways is free with the exception of toll bridges. Seat belts are required at all times; litter laws are strictly enforced. It is a good idea to pick up a book on driving rules in California.

The **speed limit** throughout the state on the freeways is 88 kph (55 mph), with some exceptions in rural areas, and is frequently posted in all other areas. Keep to these limits as patrol cars won't hesitate to pull you over.

Sign posting is generally very clear, but have with you a good map with you and plan your route beforehand. If you go wrong on a busy freeway, it can be very difficult to correct yourself. Again, it may be a good idea to carry with you a book on driving rules and sign interpretations.

Parking restrictions should be strictly adhered to. RED CURBS mean no parking; YELLOW CURBS mean restricted loading permitted only; WHITE CURBS mean short-term parking; GREEN CURBS mean limited parking and the time limit will be indicated; BLUE CURBS are for disabled parking only. Watch out for tow-away zones as they mean what they say.

Petrol (gas) is much cheaper than in Europe. Credit cards are accepted. Most gas stations are service stations. Your windscreen will be washed and your oil checked if you ask.

Hitchhiking

Hitchhiking is legal, except on expressways and parkways, but it really is not advisable. As in many countries, it is not particularly safe and for that same reason many drivers are loath to pick up hitchhikers.

Accommodation

Throughout California there is a huge range of quality accommodation (recommended places to stay listed by area can be found beginning on page 321). It is always a good idea to book in advance to make sure you get what you want. For **hotels** and **motels,** cost is usually per room, not per occupant, and rates may be subject to state tax. You will probably have the choice between a twin room (two beds) or a double room (one bed for two people). Two double beds are ideal if you are travelling in a family. The bigger, more prestigious hotels, often found in well-known areas of the city, usually offer transport to and from the airport, facilities to book for events such as the theatre, restaurant recommendations, and can be very helpful in guiding you around the area. Always make the most of local recommendations. There are many motel chains, such as Howard Johnson or Quality Inn, which are easily located along the highways, are very convenient and are reasonably priced. Most offer a restaurant or similar place to eat, television and private bath, and very often a swimming pool.

Around the smaller communities and holiday areas, **guest houses** and **bed and breakfasts** are usually available; lists of these can be obtained from the local tourist office. **Country inns** are particularly popular in central and northern California. They are usually relatively small and personal, comfortable and well situated, though they may be rather more basic than the hotels. It is best to book in advance. **Hostels** are usually quite comfortable and always very cheap. They are best suited to those who really do not mind sleeping "a bit rough", that is dormitory-style, or helping with the general maintenance of the establishment. **Youth hostels** are open to those who belong to national youth hostel organizations overseas. You do not have to be a member of the YMCA to stay at one of their locations, but it is best to book well in advance.

Camping throughout California can mean anything from tents to RVs (recreational vehicles) and the variety of places to camp are limitless, such as beach areas, national parks, state parks, forests and monuments. Facilities provided also vary. Some offer hook-ups to electricity and water, laundry facilities, toilets, restaurants, shops, swimming pools and children's play areas. It is best to book well in advance as camping is very popular. You can receive a list of campsites around the state or country from: Kampgrounds of America, PO Box 30162, Billings, Montana, 59114.

Travelling with Children

California is the perfect place to take children. There is so much designed for their enjoyment (and geared towards those adults who want to be children!). There are so many activities, fun and educational, and types of holidays that no child, no matter what age, would ever be bored. Many motels do not charge for children under 12 and menus often offer a selection especially for children. If you are travelling with children, make a point of checking with the local tourist office or your hotel for suggested children's activities in the area. Many educational and fun things to do are completely free.

Language

English is the official language in the United States, although Spanish is heard throughout California.

Drinking

To consume alcohol in the State of California you must be at least 21 years of age.

Communication Services

Telephones
Public telephones are easily located and you need exact change, in 5, 10 and 25 cent pieces, in order to make a call. Calling the operator by dialling "0" is free. For local information call 411. For toll-free information call (0800) 555-1212. All numbers with an "0800" preceding the number are free of charge. For information outside of your locality, dial the respective area code followed by 555-1212 free of charge. Long-distance and international calls can be dialled direct but if calling from a public telephone box

make sure you have plenty of change! Some credit cards may also be used when making a call, but check with the operator first.

Telegrams
Telegram companies, such as Western Union and International Telephone and Telegraph (ITT) are listed in the Yellow Pages or in the local telephone directory, or phone (0800) 555-1212 for their office numbers. Telegrams can be charged to your hotel bill or paid direct from a public telephone box.

Post Office
Post office opening hours are from 8.30 or 9 a.m. to 5 or 5.30 p.m., Mondays to Fridays, and Saturday mornings from 8 or 9 a.m. to 12 noon or 1 p.m. These are general times, however, and some larger branches stay open longer, whereas some smaller branches have shorter hours (some stay open 24 hours a day).

Stamps may also be purchased at your hotel, and from machines in drugstores (chemists), transportation terminals and in many public places, although you pay more for these. Be sure, whenever sending mail within the United States, to include the zip code.

Emergencies

Police are, on the whole, very helpful and friendly and willing to assist whenever possible, so do not hesitate to approach a policeman for assistance. If you need to contact the police, fire, ambulance or paramedics in an emergency, dial "911", or contact the operator by dialling "0" and get put through to the service you require.

Drugstores (chemists), for less serious cases, are easily located in the local Yellow Pages or telephone information. Opening times vary, but generally drugstores are open quite late, if not 24 hours a day.

It is certainly not cheap to have **hospital** treatment anywhere in the United States, so medical insurance is essential when travelling. This cannot be emphasized enough. In fact, assistance may be refused if there is no proof of medical insurance. Hospital standards are very high (as are the costs) and most hospitals have a 24-hour emergency facility.

Clothing Sizes (dresses, blouses, knitwear)	
USA	GB
8	10/32
10	12/34
12	14/36
14	16/38
16	18/40

(Men's suits and shirt collar sizes are the same as in Europe)

roof or in one area) you can imagine. Most malls are open seven days a week and until quite late in the evening, particularly on sale days. The smaller town and city shops usually open from 10 a.m. to 5.30 or 6 p.m., Monday to Saturday.

Holidays

In California, as throughout the United States, there are only eight legal holidays when banks, government offices and some shops will be closed. They are: New Year's Day (1 January); Martin Luther King Jr. Day (the third Monday in January); Easter Sunday (March or April); Memorial Day (the fourth Monday in May); American Independence Day (4 July); Labor Day (the first Monday in September); Thanksgiving Day (the fourth Thursday in November); and Christmas Day (25 December).

Shopping

Shopping could be considered a Californian culture, and is definitely one of its favourite pastimes. Shops range from small, specialist shops to the largest malls (many shops under one

Tipping

If a service charge is not included on the bill, you are expected to tip waiters, waitresses and bartenders at least 15 per cent. Taxi drivers, hairdressers and tour guides should be tipped about the same and porters about $1 per bag.

National and State Parks

California is particularly noted for its huge areas of public land devoted to recreational and outdoor purposes. All through the state you will find numerous national parks, national forests, monuments and recreational areas, not to mention state historical monuments, nature reserves, beaches, state parks, campsites and recreation areas open to the public. Some areas within the national park, forest and state parks system charge a small amount for entrance or day use.

Climate

The climate and weather conditions throughout California vary tremendously. In southern California the climate varies between the desert, the beaches, the valleys and the mountains. Along the coastal regions, seasons do not change very much. Summers are warm with varying humidity, although during August and September the smog is at its worst in Los Angeles. Winters are mild and the rainy season lasts from January to March.

Dress, on the whole, is casual and the evenings tend to cool down, particularly in the winter, so carry a sweater or jacket with you. Desert areas can reach well over 40°C (100°F), whereas mountain regions can be very cold indeed. As you travel north along the coast into central and northern California, the temperature becomes cooler. San Francisco daytime temperatures average during the summer months around 15°C (59°F), which is quite cool. The spring and autumn months are often warmer, sometimes reaching over 27°C (into the 80s°F). The valley areas of Sacramento and San Joaquin are the hottest regions, often over 32°C (into the 90s°F) during the summer. Fog along the coast is particularly common during the summer, although it does burn off by midday, and the rainy season is generally from December until the end of February. It is a good idea, no matter what time of year you are travelling through central and northern California, to carry a sweater and light coat, particularly for the evenings. Dress, again, is quite casual, and in San Francisco you will see just about every kind of dress imaginable. The most important item to remember is sensible walking shoes.

California Average Temperatures Fahrenheit/Celsius						
	JAN	MARCH	MAY	JULY	SEPT	NOV
Anaheim	52/11	57/14	64/17	72/22	70/21	59/15
Eureka	47/8	49/9	53/11	56/13	56/13	52/11
Lake Tahoe	27/-3	34/1	48/9	62/17	55/13	37/3
Los Angeles	56/13	58/14	63/17	71/21	70/21	62/17
Monterey	48/9	52/11	58/14	62/16	61/16	52/11
Mt. Shasta	33/1	42/5	53/12	67/19	60/16	42/6
Palm Springs	55/13	63/17	76/24	91/32	84/29	64/17
Sacramento	46/8	55/12	64/18	74/23	71/21	54/12
San Diego	55/13	59/14	62/16	68/20	68/20	61/16
San Francisco	50/10	55/12	57/14	59/15	62/16	57/14
Santa Barbara	53/11	56/13	60/16	66/19	66/19	59/15
Yosemite	35/2	45/7	57/14	71/21	64/17	44/7

A Country within a Country— California is the Golden State

Many Europeans travelling to California may return saying that the only thing missing is history. All right, it's true; this massive state, once considered an untamed wilderness, was only discovered in 1542, and was then essentially ignored for the following 200 years. It didn't even become part of the Union until 1850. But crammed within this relatively short period of time have been an abundance of dreams, stubbornness, determination, bravery and beliefs that built a wild frontier into a country within a country.

History

On 28 September 1542, the Portuguese explorer Juan Ròdrigez Cabrillo, commander of two Spanish vessels, landed off the coast of California. Travelling from Mexico and heading for Spain, he dropped anchor in a beautiful and sheltered bay he named San Miguel and claimed the territory for Spain. Today, it is called San Diego. From there, he continued north along the

A photographer's dream—no matter what time of day or year, California provides ever-changing scenes. No wonder artists find the coastline inspirational.

coast, dying *en route*, and, as his companions were not terribly impressed by what they found, they returned home to Spain. Thirty-seven years later, in 1579, the English sea captain, Sir Francis Drake, travelled north along the coast in search of the North-west Passage. He landed somewhere near Monterey (where, exactly, no one is absolutely certain) claiming the territory for England. Then he, too, returned home.

Drake's claim on northern California did arouse some interest in the Spaniards who had paid little attention to their own discovery, but it wasn't until 1769 that the Spanish soldier and newly appointed Governor of California, Captain Gaspar de Portola, returned to occupy the territory and to secure his country's claim. Up until

The Central Coast, with all its immense beauty and tremendous variety, continues to attract visitors all the year round.

that time, Native Americans lived here simply and peacefully. Tribes such as the Maidu, Hupa and Mojave led almost separate existences, cut off from one another by the inaccessible mountains and vast, unwelcoming deserts.

From San Diego, Portola travelled north and established his second

The Founding of the Missions

San Diego de Alcalá (San Diego), 16 July 1769

San Carlos Borromeo de Carmelo (Carmel) 3 June 1770

San Antonio de Padua (near Jolon) 14 July 1771

San Gabriel Archangel (San Gabriel) 8 September 1771

San Luis Obispo de Tolosa (San Luis Obispo) 1 September 1772

San Francisco de Asis (San Francisco) 9 October 1776

San Juan Capistrano (San Juan Capistrano) 1 November 1776

Santa Clara de Asis (Santa Clara) 12 January 1777

San José de Guadalupe (Fremont) 11 July 1779

San Buenaventura (Ventura) 31 March 1782

Santa Bárbara (Santa Barbara) 4 December 1786

La Purisima Concepcion (near Lompoc) 8 December 1787

Santa Cruz (Santa Cruz) 28 August 1791

Nuestra Señora de la Soledad (near Soledad) 9 October 1791

San Juan Bautista (San Juan Bautista) 24 June 1797

San Miguel Archangel (San Miguel) 25 July 1797

San Fernando Rey de España (San Fernando) 8 September 1797

San Luis Rey de Francia (near Oceanside) 13 June 1798

Santa Inés (Solvang) 17 September 1804

San Rafael Archangel (San Rafael) 14 December 1817

San Francisco de Solano (Sonoma) 4 July 1823

Portola led an expedition that established military forts in San Diego (which had been so named by the Spanish explorer Sebastian Vizcaino in 1602) and the following year further north in Monterey. With Portola travelled the Franciscan friar, Junipero Serra, who had been chosen to lead the movement that was to establish the Franciscan Order in California. Serra became known as the Apostle of California and, led by Portola, he and his missionaries set out to christianize the Native Americans and to establish the extraordinary mission chain of California. Imagine, more than two centuries ago, a group of men travelling across an unexplored and wild land wearing only grey robes and sandals and carrying with them only the barest of supplies. They brought the Native American Indians into their faith and with their help, on 16 July 1769, founded the first of the 21 missions on Presido Hill, San Diego, and named it San Diego de Alcalá. There is tremendous controversy over the treatment of the Native Americans by the Franciscans and the diseases that white man brought with him from across the ocean, killing the Natives by the thousands. But without the hard work and knowledge of the Natives, the Franciscans' task would have been hard to complete.

MISSIONS

N

SONOMA
SAN RAFAEL
San Francisco
DOLORES SAN JOSE
SANTA CLARA
SANTA CRUZ
SAN JUAN BAUTISTA
CARMEL SOLEDAD 99
SAN ANTONIO
SAN MIGUEL
SAN LUIS OBISPO
LA PURISIMA SANTA INES
SANTA BARBARA
SAN BUENAVENTURA SAN FERNANDO
Los Angeles SAN GABRIEL
SAN JUAN CAPISTRANO PALA
SAN LUIS REY
SAN DIEGO
San Diego

PACIFIC OCEAN

✝ Missions

0 ——— 50 km
0 ——— 30 miles

*T*he Californian mission chain.

In 1822, Mexico won its independence from Spain, and California became a province of Mexico, forcing the Franciscan friars to return home to Spain (as they refused allegiance to Mexico), leaving their valuable mission land to be dispersed at the government's discretion. Converted Native Americans scattered and the mission buildings were left to decay.

In 1826, Jedediah Strong Smith, a trapper, became the first American to reach California by land, via the Sierra Nevada Mountains. As word spread across the country that this wilderness really was accessible, and was so much bigger than anyone ever imagined, more and more Americans braved the sea and land journey and began to settle in this Mexican province. It wasn't long before the American settlers realized the potential value of the

military fort at the site of Monterey and, in 1770, the Franciscans founded the second of the missions—San Carlos Borromeo de Carmelo (Carmel)— nearby. It was from the hills above Carmel, while searching for Monterey, that Portola sighted the magnificent San Francisco Bay that had been missed by explorers and navigators for 200 years.

Six years later, the same year as the American War of Independence, the first groups of Spanish settlers began to arrive. They sailed into the San Francisco Bay, where they founded a presidio and the Mission San Francisco de Asis (Dolores) and established villages, called pueblos, along the coast. By 1823, all 21 missions were founded from San Diego to Sonoma.

Spanish California

For more than 50 years after the Portola expeditions, California remained a Spanish colony. Many of the Spanish settlers acquired a great deal of land from the Spanish government and, with Native American labour, became very wealthy farmers and ranchers. It wasn't until 1796 that the first American sailing vessel landed on the Californian coast, anchoring in Monterey. From then on, American trading to the missions and harbours flourished as the boats worked their way up and down the coast.

land but the Mexican government refused to sell any of it to the American government. On 13 May 1846 President James Polk declared war on Mexico. Events tended to overtake one another at this time as news took so long to travel the great distance from the seat of government in Washington DC. So at about the same time, settlers just north of San Francisco, unaware that war was brewing, stormed the Sonoma estate of General Mariano Vallejo and raised, in defiance, a handmade version of the bear flag, now the flag of California, which carried the words "California Republic". A brave gesture, but the idea of an independent republic was soon dropped once war was declared. In 1848, Mexico surrendered its claim to the province and California became a territory of the United States. In 1850, California became the 31st state in the Union.

The year 1848 marks another very important development in Californian history: the discovery of gold. James Wilson Marshall, while building a sawmill for John A. Sutter on the south fork of the American River in the Sierra Nevada foothills near Sacramento, picked up some shiny rocks from the river. News of the discovery of gold spread across the country like wildfire and the famous California Gold Rush began. What had been up until then a slow trickle of settlers making their way across to the West soon became a flood of eager and greedy gold-diggers, from all over the world, desperate to make their fortunes. They became know as the Forty-Niners. Within a year, more than 80,000 had flocked to the Gold Country, the start of the rush that

within 12 years raised the white population of California from about 5,000 to 380,000.

Towns and cities appeared overnight, flourished and just as quickly disappeared again leaving ghostly relics. Cities such as Sacramento and San Francisco grew at a tremendous rate and suffered for it. As fast as a state government and state politics were being formed, many of the Forty-Niners took the law very much into their own hands and towns ran riot. Within just a few years, the population of San Francisco rose from under 1,000 to over 30,000, a rate of growth faster than that of any other city in the country. The city was filled with gambling halls, brothels, corruption and greed. Many people did make their fortunes. In 1850 alone some $40 million worth of gold had been mined. Those who invested their money wisely in land and businesses benefited; some found gold and returned home, while others not so successful continued down into the Central Valley and took up farming and ranching or travelled further north and turned their skills to lumbering and fishing. When the Gold Rush balloon began to deflate around 1853, the population of central California had exploded.

Now there was a tremendous need for a transcontinental railroad to open California up to the rest of the country. A brilliant engineer by the name of Theodore Dehone Judah, who had built the first railroad in the state in 1856, from Sacramento to Folsom, knew it was possible to build a railroad across the rugged mountain passes but, unfortunately for Judah, it was the four investors in the project that benefited: Mark Hopkins, Charles Crocker, Collis Huntington and Leland Stanford—later to become known as the "Big Four". The Central Pacific Railroad was completed in 1869, linking up with the rest of the country at Promontory Point, Utah, with the labour of thousands of immigrant Chinese known as "Coolies". The Big Four became very rich and powerful men.

Although trading in California was opened up in earnest, depression hit. The West couldn't compete with the East Coast prices and the railroad failed to bring the prosperity it had promised. Immigrants continued to come in droves, though work was hard to find and land prices dropped dramatically. When the Bank of California was forced to close its doors on 26 April 1875, California was at its lowest ebb. Central California turned its hopes to farming and agriculture. Farmers in the rich land of the Central Valley developed their ranches for dairy and cattle farming and grew fields of cotton, wheat and rice for valuable cash crops. Germans and other Europeans from wine-producing areas settled in the Napa and Sonoma Valleys and began producing wines from the grapes grown on vine cuttings they brought from Europe; others turned their experience to fishing and fruit harvesting. Scandinavians moved into northern California to work as lumberjacks and Japanese came in large numbers as migratory agricultural workers and tradesmen. Despite the initial depression, the population of central California continued to expand at a great rate and new towns began to emerge and grow.

Sacramento was founded in 1839 by Captain John A. Sutter on a land grant from Mexico. The settlement, known as New Helvetia, became the first outpost of white civilization in inland California. By 1848, the new town of Sacramento was laid out and Sutter's fort, nearby, was to become the western terminal of the wagon trains of the early western pioneers. Sacramento flourished during the Gold Rush (the first gold was discovered at Sutter's own mill just to the east) and in 1850 the first California legislature incorporated it as a city and the site of its first assembly.

In 1854, Sacramento was made the capital of California. San Francisco, just to the west, had experienced the worst of the corruption and greed brought by the Gold Rush, so in some ways that fateful morning on 18 April 1906 was a blessing.

The great earthquake and fire marked a new beginning for this beautiful city. The earthquake that shook the city sent shock waves from San Juan Bautista to Fort Bragg, but it was the fire that followed, ravishing the city for the next three days, that totally destroyed the city. Wooden buildings that had been hastily built during the booming years all but disappeared and 400,000 were left homeless. The city was brought to the ground. Here was an opportunity to start afresh, to build the proud city as it deserved to be built and elect new leaders for the task. In 1915, the Panama-Pacific International Exposition opened in celebration of the rebirth of San Francisco.

Southern California emerged in its own right during the 20th century separately from the north. Initially, during the 19th century, the area was settled by farmers attracted by the excellent climate and rich soil that promised a great wealth in farming and agriculture, particularly cotton, alfalfa and fruits. As the railroads stretched across the United States, produce could travel the great distances across country and still reach the markets fresh.

The only thing southern California lacked was fresh water, but aqueducts, reservoirs and wells were built to preserve the little they had and to transport water also down from further north.

The first real boom began at the end of the 19th century when oil was discovered by Edward L. Doheny in the Los Angeles area, followed by other areas along the coast and up through the hills. Although the oil boom encouraged a whole new stream of settlers into the area, it was just a few years later, as the 20th century began to emerge and the magic of the motion picture was first realized, that southern California was really put on the map.

The movie industry exploded as film makers were attracted to the area by the consistently good climate, available space to build their huge sprawling studios and a wide selection of natural outdoor "sets" all within easy reach. Movie hopefuls with dreams of stardom arrived from all over the world. Writers saw their opportunities also and as silent pictures finally gave way to the "talkies" there was no holding back. Today, southern California is still the motion picture capital of the world.

Geography and Geology

California is the third largest state in the nation, after Texas and Alaska, and totals 411,048 km² (158,706 square miles) with 3,108 km (1,200 miles) of Pacific coastline. In the east and to the west are high mountain ranges which are joined together at the northern and southern ends by shorter ranges. Running in between the two higher ranges is the Central Valley, which resembles a plain, and to the south lies a combination of desert, fertile valleys, mountains and coastal plains.

Geographically and topographically, southern California, which is divided from central and northern California by the Tehachapi Mountains, is one of the most varied regions in the United States. Where else can one sunbathe on gorgeous sandy beaches and then travel just a few hours to ski on snow-topped mountains? Or, where else can one find dry, desolate deserts lying alongside rich and fertile agricultural land? The mountain ranges, though not as high as those found further north, are spectacular, and the valleys that nestle between these mountains are very fertile, producing an abundance of crops including citrus and semi-tropical fruits. It is fully understandable that the early explorers of the 17th century believed California to be an island, as the mountains, valleys and plains cut them off from easy exploration.

Southern California can be divided into eight separate counties. The county of San Bernardino, east of Los Angeles, is the largest county in the United States. As a tourist was heard to say, while standing at Point Loma in San Diego: on a clear day, if you look straight out, you can see Japan! Well, not quite, but you would be looking towards the Far East. Where the Pacific Ocean meets California, it produces one of the most beautiful coastlines in the world. The ocean water along the southern part of the coast comes up from the south and is clean and mild throughout the year. It is the perfect all-year-round water playground with its cool breezes for sailing and windsurfing, spectacular waves for surfing, and clear, deep waters for fishing and scuba-diving. Sandy bays, craggy inlets and sheltered coves run one into the other, making the coastline of southern California one of the most picturesque and sought-after places to live. Probably one of the most spectacular views out to sea is that of the migrating grey whale which travels south to Baja California during December and January and north again to the cold Alaskan waters during March and April.

The mountain ranges of southern California are perhaps not as high as those found further north, but a few peaks, such as San Gorgonio and Mount Pinos, rise to an altitude of around 2,700–3,000 m (9,000–10,000 ft) above sea level. The Tehachapi Mountains form the dividing line between southern California and the Central Valley and mountain ranges of the north. Smaller mountains, which include the Santa Monica, San Bernardino and San Gabriel, are part of the range that runs east from Point Conception, north of Los Angeles. Mountains such as the Santa Ana and Laguna Mountains form the Peninsular Ranges that run south along the coast into Baja California.

Say "desert" and we think of miles and miles of empty sand that leads to nowhere, a lonely place where no one would wish to go. But the desert area in the south-east of the state, vast and awe-inspiring as it is, is a paradise in itself. The desert region lies 225 km (140 miles) to the east of San Diego and 172 km (107 miles) east of Los Angeles and is neither entirely desolate nor barren. Resort communities, hotels and year-round sports facilities make much of the region a sought-after vacationing area. Wildlife, flora and fauna, picturesque landscapes and fresh, clean air are irresistible attractions for anyone in search of untouched beauty and tranquillity.

The desert region is split into two: the Colorado Desert (or lower desert) to the south, extending to the Mexican border, and the High Mojave Desert (pronounced moh-HAH-vay) which stretches east to the state of Nevada and well up into central California. The Colorado Desert includes the Anza-Borrego Desert State Park; the Salton Sea, a 7,290-hectare (18,000-acre) wildlife refuge and state park lying within the Imperial Valley; the Coachella Valley, which millions of year ago lay at the bottom of the sea and is now the home of nine luxurious desert resort communities such as Palm Springs; and the Joshua Tree Monument, a wildlife sanctuary covering more than 2,250 km² (870 square miles) east of Los Angeles. The Mojave Desert includes the Death Valley National Monument, 836,837 hectares (2,067,795 acres), the third largest national monument in the United States.

Riding through the desert of Palm Springs is just one of the many family activities to be enjoyed.

This arid desert basin east of Santa Barbara, is the lowest point in the United States—86 m (282 ft) below sea level at its lowest point—and the hottest area on the North American continent.

Along the eastern border of central California lies the Sierra Nevada Mountain range, an extremely high and steep wall of rock. At more than 640 km (400 miles) long and about 110 km (70 m) wide, it forms the backbone of California. Several of the peaks along this range rise more than 4,300 m (14,000 ft) feet above sea level and the tallest peak of all, Mount Whitney, at 4,418 m (14,495 ft) is the highest in the United States outside

Alaska. Lying in the heart of the Sierra Nevada is the extraordinarily beautiful wilderness of Yosemite National Park, a nationally protected area filled with forest, canyons, lakes, rivers, gorges and waterfalls, including the famous Yosemite Falls, the highest in North America. Further south in the Sierra Nevada are the adjacent Sequoia and Kings Canyon National Parks, home to the giant sequoia trees, the largest living things.

A chain of smaller mountain ranges lie along the Pacific Ocean, known as the Coast Range. This range is divided up, each part with its own name, such as the Santa Cruz and the Santa Lucia, varying in width from 32 km (20 miles) to 64 km (40 miles) and in height ranging from 610 m (2,000 ft) to 2,440 m (8,000 ft) above sea level. The ridges that divide the coastal ranges enclose many beautiful and fertile valleys and woodlands. The state of

California has more Pacific coastline than the states of both Washington and Oregon put together—a total of 19,300 km (12,000 miles)—and it is along the coastal regions that a great wealth of natural resources has existed. Oil, natural gas, salt, mercury, sulphur and manganese, and other valuable minerals have been found here. Beautiful bays, inlets and coves line the coast, from the sandy beaches in the south to the rugged and wooded shoreline to the north. The diversity of landform is breathtaking

The vast, fertile Central Valley, California's agricultural heartland, that runs in between these two long mountain ranges, is more than 720 km (450 miles) in length and averages 64 km (40 miles) in width. It is anchored to the north by Redding and to the extreme south by Bakersfield. The valley can actually be divided into two: one half formed by the Sacramento River and the other formed by the San Joaquin River. Except in the extreme south, the land here is naturally very fertile and is a very important farming and agricultural area. It is known as the agricultural "cornucopia" of the United States and contains about three-fifths of the agricultural land in California. Fruits, nuts, vegetables and livestock are the staples of production.

The northern third of the state is the least populated and most unspoilt region in California. The coastline is

The spectacular natural wonders of Yosemite still invoke gasps of disbelief and amazement from visitors as they have done for centuries.

rugged, the mountains dramatic and the forests awe-inspiring. Inland, Mount Shasta towers above six national forests of pine, cedar and oak, five glaciers and eight national and state parks. Lassen Volcanic National Park can be found in the Shasta-Cascade region. The Cascades run to the north from California to British Columbia in Canada and in California cover about 80 km (50 miles) across. Lassen Peak, at a height of 3,187 m (10,457 ft) is one of the two volcanoes in the Cascades to have erupted this century (the other one being Mount St Helens, which erupted in 1980).

Climate

Southern California has one of the most ideal climates in the world and one of the more variable. It is often considered a "country by itself" when it comes to weather, in that it has a type of climate found nowhere else in the United States. The area along the coast is mild all year round, tempered by a constant cool breeze coming off the Pacific. Average temperatures in San Diego range from 18°C (64°F) in the winter to 25°C (77°F) in the summer. A light rainy season can be expected between November and March. During the summer months, the humidity is low so the climate is comfortable, but it is important to note, when listening to a weather forecast, how clean the air is rated. The famous Los Angeles smog can be particularly bad during August and September.

Venture inland from the consistently mild climate of the coast and you find the tremendously variable temperatures

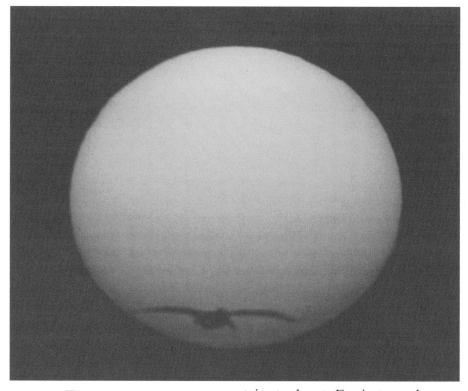

*P*eace and tranquillity.

of the desert and mountains. The desert areas are some of the hottest in the world, with summer temperatures that often reach around 54°C (130°F). However, if you travel just a short distance to the mountain areas you can experience heavy rainfall and, on the higher peaks, winter snow. There is nowhere else in the United States where you can surf and ski in the space of one day!

The climate through central and northern California varies dramatically from south to north and from moun-

tains to desert. For instance, because of the high altitude of the Sierra Nevada, this is the coldest part of the state where freezing temperatures can occur during the summer months. Snow covers some of the peaks all year round and winters are long and often severe. Temperatures along the coast are consistently mild all year round, tempered by the winds off the Pacific. Temperatures in San Francisco, for instance, average 12–14°C (mid-50s °F), a sort of perpetual spring, with the warmest months being September and October. Summer months can be quite cool. Only the valley areas such as Sacramento experience high summer temperatures of about 32°C (90°F). Rainfall increases from south to north, the rainy season being between

November and March. Average annual rainfall in, say, San Francisco, is about 51 cm (20 in). Continue to travel north and the average rainfall increases significantly. Coastal fog which appears though the summer will usually burn off by the middle of the day, although evening fog in San Francisco is quite common.

Nationalities and Politics

The United States has always been considered a "hotchpotch" of different nationalities, and no less so California, though its history of growth is more recent. What began as a mixture of Spanish colonialism and American romanticism soon became a melting-pot of dreams from around the world.

Southern California has always been greatly influenced by neighbouring Mexico. Today, this is evident in the bright colours, art, cuisine and language of Mexico that can be seen, tasted and heard all over the area. Many Mexicans, both legal and illegal, continue to come over the border in search of work and a better standard of living. During the 19th century, many thousands of Chinese "coolies" were imported to build the railroads and remained to work the farms, be house servants or set up their own businesses. Today, the Chinese population is still high, especially in cities like Los Angeles and San Francisco, where Chinatown, in the heart of the city, is the largest Asian community outside the Orient. The Japanese also have come over in large numbers to work the land and to fish, but the

*L*ake Shastina in Siskiyou County provides the perfect setting for golfing enthusiasts—summer recreation with a winter backdrop.

most recent large-scale immigration from the east is from Vietnam and Korea. There are also many American Indian Reserves in southern California where Native Americans continue to farm, raise cattle and preserve their national heritage.

It is only since the beginning of this century that southern California boomed with the immigration of Americans from other states. It began with farming and the discovery of oil, then the motion picture business and the promise of a relatively untouched region where fortunes could be made and hard work rewarded. Relatively new, but unlike a city such as New York where third and fourth generation Europeans still hold on very much to their old-world heritage, native-born Americans living in California are very much Californian. Everyone has an international background, be it English, German, Irish or Russian, but ask them where they come from and they will say "California".

The United States and the world travelled into central and northern California to make their fortunes much earlier, and if they didn't find it in the gold or silver, they ventured further afield and turned their knowledge and experience to business, farming, lumber, ranching or fishing. Europeans discovered the perfect environment for establishing vineyards, while others took to lumberjacking and dairy farming. Mexicans and Filipinos worked as labourers and on the farms, and Russians fished all along the coast and ventured inland for fur trapping.

Politically, and now with the largest population of any state in the country, California has always been very active, especially on the university campuses, and it enjoys a powerful national voice. Because it has one of the largest university systems in the United States, it has always had a tremendous amount of youthful political awareness and energy and has fought hard for contemporary issues particularly during the 1960s.

During Second World War, San Francisco and the surrounding areas probably played a greater role in the

*S*an Francisco, once the hippie capital of the world, has always been a city that attracts individuals doing their individual things.

Pacific war than any other city in the United States. The ports were constantly busy. San Francisco became the largest ship-building centre in the world and the site of the largest base in the United States Army. This period marked a new flood of immigration into the area as war jobs were abundant. The war ended and, as families began to settle back to normal life, new attitudes among the young began to emerge. First, during the 1950s, it was the beatniks. According to the Universal Dictionary, they were "persons whose dress and behaviours showed pointed, often exaggerated, disregard for conventional norms". Not a terribly significant phase, although their total disregard for everything America believed in sent shock waves through the country. It was the New Left and the hippies, emerging in California during the 1960s, who had a significant effect on American attitudes.

If any one area stands out above all the others as an activist and initiator of free thinking, it is San Francisco. Because of the wave of immigration during the mid-19th century, California has always attracted the anti-conformist and the free-thinker. During the 1960s San Francisco became the centre of hippie revolution and California became filled with young people who protested love and peace, pro-drugs and anti-war. The New Left, on the other hand, were more aggressive. The nucleus of this politically active phase in American history was the universities, particularly the University of California at Berkeley. They brought anti-racism to the forefront, they forced America to look at itself and its involvement in Vietnam, they fought against affluence and materialism, for Black Rights and for freedom of speech and free thinking. As hippies became fashionable around the world, so too were the New Left heard. They shocked the country at the time but they did, without a doubt, change American thinking.

As the state capital, Sacramento is the centre of Californian government. The state of California is governed under a constitution that was adopted in 1879, although amended many times, by executive officers elected by the state for a period of four years. Executive officers consist of a Governor, Secretary of State, Controller, Treasurer, Attorney General and Superintendent of Public Instruction. Local government, that is the governments of the counties, cities and towns, receive their power from the State Government.

Many famous politicians made their start in California, but probably the best-known Governor of California to emerge in recent years is former President Ronald Reagan. Former President Richard Nixon was born in Yoba Linda, southern California, and Earl Warren, the 14th Chief Justice of the United State Supreme Court, was born in Los Angeles and served as State Governor for three consecutive terms.

The People, Culture and Lifestyles

Southern Californian lifestyle revolves very much around its open attitude of "you can do whatever you want", and its consistently mild climate that allows you to do whatever you want all the year round. And there is a very fine line between lifestyle and culture. Take Los Angeles for instance. We think of the lifestyles of the rich and famous, Beverly Hills, stretch limousines and swimming pools and the culture of the motion picture and music business. But there is more. Los Angeles offers excellent theatre, opera, ballet and art, museums and galleries, not to mention buzzing ethnic and seaside communities, great dining and unlimited shopping.

Orange County is a good example of the diversity of interests in southern California. Disneyland is very much a part of American culture and is only a short distance from one of the most technically advanced centres for the performing arts in the world. Travel further south to San Diego and although the stress of life is slower than in its neighbouring Los Angeles, the desire to be physically active picks up. Lifestyles and culture revolve around the outdoors with year-round sports and recreational activities, concerts and theatre, museums and art exhibitions.

The large number of universities and colleges in southern California are also important cultural centres. In their own communities (and a university such as UCLA which, with a student population of about 30,000, really is a community in itself) they offer all types of recreational and cultural activities made available to everyone, from football to innovative theatre.

Generally, it can be said that those who live in central and northern California do so because they love it.

Polo in the desert. Some of the best polo teams in the world can be seen competing in Palm Springs.

Many artists and writers choose to live in this part of the state because it's inspirational and there's a calmness and beauty that brings you closer to nature. It is, dare it be said, more down-to-earth than southern California, less fabricated, more historic and more cultural, with a deep sense of what is real. On this subject, southern California and the rest of the state would rather go their separate ways. The people are very friendly and proud of where they live, even if they haven't lived there very long. Cities such as San Francisco and Sacramento have an elegance and style about them. The residents are

*E*agle Lake—an *immense but peaceful setting for those who want to get away from it all.*

sophisticated and cosmopolitan with an easy-going attitude and a broad-minded approach to life. Altogether, they are welcoming because they understand well the feeling that those who visit want to stay forever.

Festivals and Events

A huge variety of festivals and events occur throughout the state. Chances are, whenever you are travelling, you will experience a Californian festivity. Here is a list of the bigger and better known events, but be sure to stop and ask either at your hotel or visitors' information centre for additional activities and exact dates within the area.

January
Tournament of the Roses Parade and Rose Bowl Game—Pasadena, Los Angeles.
Annual Tournament of Gold Champions—San Diego.

The National Orange Show in San Bernardino is the location of not only a very popular off-track betting facility but also the annual spring show and carnival.

Annual Martin Luther King Day Parade—San Diego.
Martin Luther King Birthday Celebration—San Francisco.
Mozart Birthday Fête—San Luis Obispo.
Bull, Gelding, Working Dog and Mule Sale—Red Bluff.
Country, Bluegrass, Fiddlers' Music Festival—Blythe.

February
Golden Dragon Parade, Chinese New Year Celebrations—Los Angeles.
Wild flowers Bloom in the Desert (Feb–April)—San Diego.
Chinese New Year and Food Fair—San Diego.
Chinese New Year Celebration (Feb/Mar)—San Francisco.
Clam Chowder Cook-off and Chowder Chase—Santa Cruz.
National Date Festival—Indio.
World Championship Crab Contests—Crescent City.
Whiskey Flat Days—Kernville.
Monterey Hot Air Affair—Laguna Seca.

March

San Juan Capistrano "Return of the Swallows" Festival—San Juan Capistrano Mission.
The Academy Awards—Los Angeles.
Avenue of the Stars St Patrick's Day Parade—Los Angeles.
Ocean Beach Kite Festival—San Diego.
La Jolla Easter Hat Parade (Mar/April)—La Jolla.
Cherry Blossom Festival (Mar/April)—Japantown, San Francisco.
Snowfest Winter Carnival—Tahoe City.
Sonoma County Folk Festival—Santa Rosa.

April

Two Week Arts Festival—Santa Barbara.
Easter Sunday Festival (Mar/April)—Los Angeles.
Long Beach Grand Prix—Los Angeles.
Coronada Flower and Garden Show—Coronada.
Wild flower Show—Pacific Grove.
National Orange Show—San Bernardino.
Toyota Grand Prix—Long Beach.
Asparagus Festival—Stockton.
North Coast's Bloomin' Best Rhododendron Festival—Eureka.

May

Escondido Avocado Festival—Escondido.
National Historic Preservation Week—San Diego.
Great California Balloon Challenge and Festival—Bakersfield.
Jumping Frog Jubilee—Angels Camp, near Sacramento.
Carnival Celebration and Parade—San Francisco.
Swedish Festival—Kingsburg.
Balloon and Wine Festival—Temecula.

June

Del Mar County Fair—Del Mar.

Greek Festival—Riverside.
Playboy Jazz Festival—Hollywood.
American Indian Fair—San Diego.
California Rodeo—Salinas, near Monterey.
San Francisco Marathon—San Francisco.
Annual Renaissance Pleasure Fair—San Bernardino.
Valley Flower Festival—Lompoc.
Huck Finn Jubilee—Victorville.

July

4 July Independence Day Parades and Festivals held throughout the state.
Malibu Arts Festival—Malibu.
Festival of the Bells—Mission San Diego de Alcala.
Carmel Bach Festival—Carmel.
World's Largest Salmon Barbecue—Fort Bragg.
Gilroy Garlic Festival—Gilroy.
Festival of Arts and Pageant of the Masters—Laguna Beach.
National Horse Show—Santa Barbara.
Sierra Nevada Old Time Fiddlers' Contest—Quincy.

August

Annual Long Beach Jazz Festival—Long Beach.
Nisei Week Japanese Festival—Little Tokyo, Los Angeles.
El Dorado County Fair—Placerville.
Serra Pageant—Carmel.
Annual Mozart Festival (July/Aug)—San Luis Obispo.
Old Spanish Days Fiesta (July/Aug)—Santa Barbara.
California State Fair—Sacramento.
Gravenstein Apple Fair—Sebastopol.

September

Mexican Independence Day and Parade—Los Angeles and San Diego.
Harbor Days Tall Ship Festival—San Diego.

Festival of the Viewing of the Moon—
Japantown, San Francisco.
Napa Wine Festival and Crafts Fair—
Napa.
Annual Harvest Festival—San Luis
Obispo.
Bear Valley Rodeo—Big Bear Lake.
Monterey Jazz Festival—Monterey.
Danish Days—Solvang.

October
Grand National Livestock Expo Rodeo
and Horse Show—San Francisco.
Great Halloween Pumpkin Festival—
San Francisco.
Desert Festival—Borrego Springs.
Annual Clam Festival—Pismo Beach.
ICS World Chilli Cook-off—Rosamond.
Annual Underwater Pumpkin Carving
Contest—La Jolla.
Italian–American Cultural Festival—
San Jose.
Silverado Days—Buena Park.

November
Death Valley Encampment—Death
Valley.
Cattle Call—Brawley.

Annual Grand Prix of Southern Cali-
fornia—Del Mar.
San Diego Thanksgiving Dixieland
Jazz Festival—San Diego.
KQED Wine and Food Festival—San
Francisco.

December
Miners' Christmas—Columbia.
Parade of Lights—Oxnard.
Christmas Boat Parade—Marina Del
Rey.
Morro Bay Lighted Boat Parade—
Morro Bay.
Mendocino Christmas Festival—Men-
docino.
Heritage House Christmas Open
House—Riverside.
Holiday in the City Parade—San Diego.
Annual Re-enactment of the Battle of
San Pasqual—Escondido.
California International Marathon—
Sacramento.

*The National Orange Show Exhibit,
San Bernardino 1913.*

38

Culturally, San Francisco stands out from any other city in the country. City residents and those who live in the vicinity need travel nowhere else, for here is offered the very best in music, theatre, ballet and the arts. There are restaurants of every description and of the highest standards and a variety of fine shopping that is more concentrated here than anywhere else. Museums and exhibitions celebrating aspects of the city they love are never-ending for everyone loves to learn, to experience and experiment and, most of all, share. This city is beautiful, and so unusual that one doesn't, in fact, even have to do anything there but look and admire.

Sacramento, the state capital, exhibits its historical culture through museums, architecture, historic districts and traditions of the Old West and its citizens show a sincere appreciation for the city's historical importance.

Sports and Recreation

Travel through California and you can't help but notice the huge variety of sports and recreational activities made available to everyone, no matter what age, sex, shape or size. Californians, on the whole, are very active people, and the comfortable and consistently warm climate of southern California and the mild temperatures further north, snow-topped mountains and huge national parks, mean that participation and spectator sports and activities can be enjoyed all year round.

In the southern part of the state, most of the action takes place along the coast. Surfing, sailing, skin-diving and scuba-diving, fishing, wind-surfing and swimming are just a few of the water sports that keep the coastline busy. Further inland, camping, walking, jogging, cycling, hiking and mountain climbing are very popular. Professional sports, such as American football, basketball, baseball, ice hockey and soccer keep the spectators happy all the year. In addition, amateur sports such as rodeos, polo, boxing, volleyball, golf and tennis, horse and car racing makes southern California a sports fanatic's haven.

For recreational activities, central and northern California also are gold mines. Along the coast, swimming, fishing, sailing, surfing and skin-diving are very popular even though the water can be very cold. Then there is camping and hiking through Yosemite National Park, Sequoia and Kings Canyon or any of the other beautiful national parks, monuments and forests; backpacking through the mountains; skiing at Heavenly Valley or Mammoth Mountain, the largest ski complexes in the United States; wine-tasting through the Napa and Sonoma Valleys; and hunting and mountain climbing. Around Lake Tahoe every recreational activity imaginable is offered, from luxury golf facilities to casinos (on the Nevada side), horseriding, hiking and camping. Northern California, a quiet, open and vast place, is a wilderness of activity. Here visitors can enjoy fishing, camping and hiking, backpacking, horseriding or Llama pack trips. California is, without a doubt, the active person's dream.

Just the Essentials

Wherever you visit, there are always too many things to see and do, particularly in California. The items on this shortlist have been selected to guide you to some of the best features in each region.

OREGON

USA

SHASTA
CASCADE

Eureka

Redding

NORTH
COAST

Reno

Placerville

Sacramento GOLD
COUNTRY

San Francisco

SAN
FRANCISCO
BAY AREA

HIGH
SIERRA

Bishop

NEVADA

CENTRAL
VALLEY

Las Vegas

PACIFIC

N

CENTRAL
COAST

Bakersfield

Barstow

DESERTS

OCEAN

Santa Barbara

GREATER
LOS
ANGELES

INLAND
EMPIRE

Los Angeles

ORANGE
COUNTY

San
Bernardino

Santa Ana

SAN
DIEGO
COUNTY

CALIFORNIA

San Diego

San Diego County
San Diego: Bazaar del mundo—
colour, music, food, life of Mexico.
Mission Bay: Sea World—fascinating,
educational fun.
Balboa Park: landscaped gardens,
interesting architecture.
San Diego Wild Animal Park: animals
roam sanctuary freely.

Orange County and the Inland Empire
San Juan Capistrano: Return of the
Swallows Festival.
Buena Park: Knott's Berry Farm.
Yorba Linda: Richard Nixon Library
and Birthplace.
Inland Empire: Hemet—Ramona
Pageant.
San Bernardino Mountains: Lake
Arrowhead—paradise for summer
activities.

Greater Los Angeles
Mann's Chinese Theater: follow the
footprints of the famous.
George C. Page Museum of La Brea
Discoveries: prehistoric fossils.
Gene Autry Western Heritage
Museum: history of American West.
Venice: trendy, friendly, eccentric.
Malibu: J. Paul Getty Museum—
Greek and Roman antiquities,
illustrated manuscripts.

The Deserts
A Colorado Desert: Anza—Borrego
Desert State Park.
Palm Springs Aerial Tramway:
spectacular view of Coachella Valley.
Joshua Tree National Monument:
wildlife sanctuary, unique ecosystem.

Central Coast
San Luis Obispo: Madonna Inn.
Farmer's market—California's largest.
Cambria: Hearst Castle—spectacular
home of a fascinating man.
Carmel: Point Lobos State Reserve—
beautiful peninsula. 17-mile drive.
Monterey Bay Aquarium: marine
research and exhibition centre.
Santa Cruz Boardwalk: old-fashioned
amusement park.

The Central Valley
Sacramento: State Capitol Building—
magnificent interior, tree park.
—Victorians—graceful homes.
Old Sacramento: Towe Ford
Automobile Museum—antique cars.
—California State Railroad
Museum—beautiful exhibition.

Gold Country
San Andreas: Calaveras County
Museum and Archives—pioneer
history.
Auburn: mining town, supply and
trading centre, stagecoach terminus.

High Sierra
Generals' Highway: connects Sequoia
and Kings Canyon National Parks.
Bishop Mule Day celebrations—best
mule show in the world—4 days.
Devil's Postpile National Monument:
amazing lava columns.
Moro Lake: three times more salty, 80
times more alkaline than the sea.

San Francisco Bay Area
Lombard Street: "world's crookedest
street".
Waterfront: Fisherman's Wharf.
Alcatraz: "The Rock".
Sausolito: waterside community.
Muir Wood National Monument:
magnificent redwoods.

North Coast
Napa Valley: Silverado trail—quiet,
scenic route through valley.
Sonoma County: Sonoma State
Historic Park.
Bodega Bay: working fishing village.
Humboldt County: Avenue of the
giants, spectacular redwoods.

Shasta Cascade
Shasta Caverns: fascinating connecting
caves made of limestone and marble.
Lassen Volcanic National Park:
bubbling mud pots, hot springs,
boiling lakes.
Castle Crags State Park: ancient
glacier polished crag towers.

41

Specific Routes Across the State with One Thing in Mind

If you are travelling through the entire state of California, the following routes have been designed for your journey, each following a specific theme, leading you through the state from south and north. And even if you are not planning any lengthy trips, but just staying in one area, use the following maps and keyed-in locations to pinpoint your particular interest.

Wine Tours

Wine-tasting and touring has become very much a part of Californian life and, although harvest time is between September and November, many wineries welcome visitors all the year round. Napa and Sonoma are considered the wine country, but those of you travelling through the state and interested in experiencing a whole range of wineries here is a general guide listed from south to north. Wine-tasting is usually free of charge and it is highly recommended to restrict winery visits to no more than four in a day.

1 TEMECULA
Growing wine centre with about 12 wineries open to the public.

2 SANTA BARBARA
Highly respected wine region concentrating mostly on white wines.

3 SAN LUIS OBISPO
Growing region producing both white and red wines.

4 SIERRA FOOTHILLS
Right in the centre of Gold Rush country a series of welcoming wineries awaits.

*Y*ou may see anything
in one of the national forests,
parks or monuments!

43

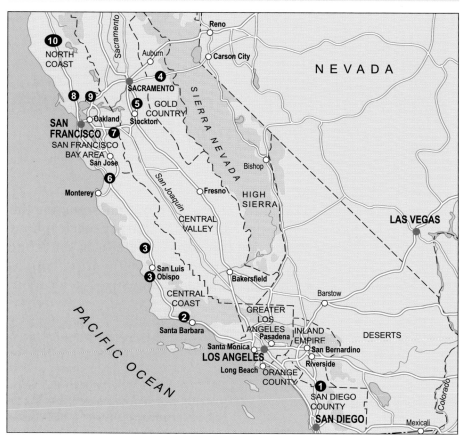

5 LODI
Small wine community producing primarily white Zinfandel.

6 HECKER PASS
Limited number of wineries producing in a relaxed country atmosphere.

7 LIVERMORE VALLEY
Small wine community specializing in white wines.

8 SONOMA COUNTY
Wide, excellent selection of wines and wineries scattered through the Sonoma Valley and further north up to Mendocino County.

Sites of selected vineyards throughout California offering wine tasting.

9 NAPA VALLEY
The most famous wine region of all, combining excellent wines, famous wineries and superb architecture.

10 MENDOCINO COUNTY
About 12 wineries open to the public specializing in white wine.

44

The California Mission Chain

The chain of 21 missions (*see* map on page 22) established through the state from San Diego in the south to Sonoma in the north were founded by the Franciscan missionaries, under the leadership of Father Junipero Serra, between 1769 and 1832. The following leisure route guide leads you from the south to the north and includes founding dates for each of the missions.

SAN DIEGO de ALCALA—1769

This was the first mission to be founded. It moved to its present site in 1774.

SAN LUIS REY de FRANCIA—1798

Once the home to over 3,000 Native Americans and still used today as a place of worship.

SAN JUAN CAPISTRANO—1776

Known as the Mission of the Swallows. Includes the Serra Chapel, the oldest building in California.

SAN GABRIEL ARCANGEL—1771

Includes the oldest cemetery in Los Angeles (1778), the burial ground of 6,000 Native Americans.

SAN FERNANDO REY de ESPANA—1796

Many interesting architectural details survive in this once-thriving community.

SAN BUENAVENTURA—1782

Original church artefacts and wooden bells can be seen on display at the museum.

SANTA BARBARA—1786

Architecturally unique and considered the "Queen of the Missions".

SANTA INES—1804

Once highly prosperous and known throughout the state for its excellent Ines Indian craft products.

LA PURISIMA CONCEPCION— 1787

The most comprehensive historical restoration in California.

SAN LUIS OBISPO de TOLOSA— 1772

Excellent collection of Mexican and Native American artefacts.

SAN MIGUEL ARCANGEL—1797

Original Native American frescoes have been fully restored in the church.

SAN ANTONIO de PADUA—1771

Fully rebuilt and restored in its unchanged and natural surroundings.

SAN CARLOS BORROMEO de CARMELO—1770

The favourite mission of Father Junipero Serra and the place of his burial.

NUESTRA SENORA de la SOLEDAD—1791

Ruins of the original building can still be seen.

SAN JUAN BAUTISTA—1797

One of the largest missions—located right on the San Andreas Fault.

SANTA CRUZ—1791

Reconstruction of the mission was

completed in 1931, approximately one-third the size of the original.

SANTA CLARA de ASIS—1777
Interior combines Spanish baroque and simple Native American designs.

SAN JOSE de GUADALUPE—1797
Only a small part of this mission was restored to its original simple yet dignified beauty.

SAN FRANCISCO de ASIS/DOLORES—1776
Relatively unchanged since its completion in 1791.

SAN RAFAEL ARCANGEL—1817
Only mission to begin life as a hospital.

SAN FRANCISCO SOLANO—1823
Life at this, the last mission to be founded in the chain, lasted only nine years—the briefest of all.

National Forests

National forests are areas set aside and supervised by the Federal Government. Many offer campsites, swimming, picnic facilities and outdoor sporting activities.

For further details, contact the US Forest Service, US Department of Agriculture, Office of Information, 630, Sansome Street, San Francisco 94111. Tel. (415) 705-2874.

1 ANGELES NATIONAL FOREST
Covers about one-quarter of Los Angeles County and includes camping, fishing, hiking, trails and winter sports.

2 CLEVELAND NATIONAL FOREST
Between Los Angeles and the Mexican border, it includes hiking, camping, fishing, trails, horseriding and hunting.

3 ELDORADO NATIONAL FOREST
Ten major lakes and reservoirs,wilderness areas, camping, fishing and boating in this High Sierra country.

4 INYO NATIONAL FOREST
Major lakes and reservoirs and mountainous terrain offer boating, fishing, hiking and camping.

5 KLAMOUTH NATIONAL FOREST
Three rivers cut through this forest area—the Klamouth, Salmon and Scott—and recreational activities include excellent fishing, white-water rafting, hiking and camping.

6 LAKE TAHOE BASIN
This, the largest alpine lake on the North American continent, offers year-round sporting activities.

7 LASSEN NATIONAL FOREST
Forest land surrounding the Lassen Volcanic National Park and offering a wide selection of recreational activities.

8 LOS PADRES NATIONAL FOREST
Divided into two separate areas—the inland area (including part of Sierra Madre Mountains) and the coastal area (including part of Big Sur).

9 MENDOCINO NATIONAL FOREST
Low mountain area in the Coast

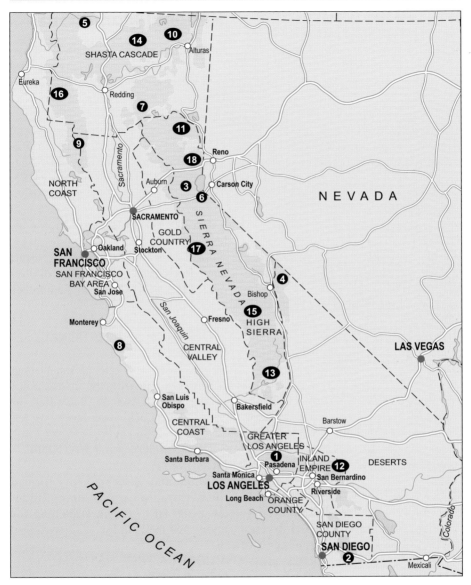

Range offering fishing, camping, hang-gliding, trails and winter sports.

10 MODOC NATIONAL FOREST
Camping, fishing, hiking, hunting, trails, swimming and winter sports are offered in this north-eastern part of the state.

California's national forests; areas set aside by the Federal Government.

11 PLUMAS NATIONAL FOREST

Three forks of the Feather River, 12 lakes and reservoirs and a wilderness area that offers boating, camping, fishing, hiking, water-skiing and hunting.

12 SAN BERNARDINO NATIONAL FOREST

Highest mountain area in southern California and one of the most popular recreational areas in the United States National Forest. Several excellent winter sports centres.

13 SEQUOIA NATIONAL FOREST

Winter and summer activities offered here in the southern Sierra Nevada.

14 SHASTA-TRINITY NATIONAL FORESTS

High peaks and low-level woodlands offering camping, hiking, houseboating, swimming and winter sports.

15 SIERRA NATIONAL FOREST

Heavily forested area on the western Sierra Nevada including two giant sequoia groves and a whole range of summer and winter activities.

16 SIX RIVERS NATIONAL FOREST

Named for the Smith, Klamouth, Trinity, Mad, Van Duzen and Eel Rivers.

17 STANISLAUS NATIONAL FOREST

Camping, fishing, hiking, horse riding, swimming, rafting and winter sports in this high mountain country.

18 TAHOE NATIONAL FOREST

Not part of Lake Tahoe but includes Sierra Nevada High Country and lower foothills.

National Monuments

National monuments are areas of historic, scientific or scenic interest that have been set aside. They are all administered by the National Park Service.

For further information contact the National Park Service, Western Regional Information Office, Fort Mason, Blvd. 201, San Francisco 94123. Tel. (415) 556-4122/(415) 556-0560.

1 CABRILLO NATIONAL MONUMENT

Named after the Portuguese explorer, Juan Rodrigez Cabrillo who, discovered THE POINT on 28 September 1542.

2 DEATH VALLEY NATIONAL MONUMENT

Desert basin and one of the hottest places on earth with the lowest point in the United States: Badwater, at 86 m (282 ft) below sea level.

3 DEVIL'S POSTPILE NATIONAL MONUMENT

Volcanic and glacier activity formed these extraordinary columns about 24 m (80 ft) high and stretching for about 400 m (¼ mile).

4 JOSHUA TREE NATIONAL MONUMENT

Desert region named after the distinctive Joshua Tree.

5 LAVA BEDS NATIONAL MONUMENT

Site of the 1872–73 Modoc Indian War and an area filled with interesting volcanic features.

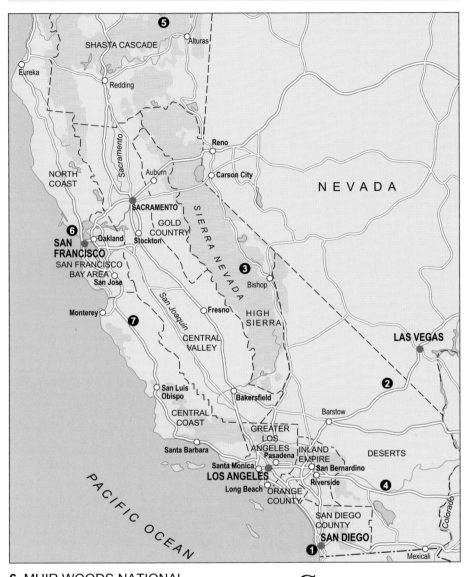

6 MUIR WOODS NATIONAL MONUMENT
Coastal redwoods at the foot of the Mount Tamalpais.

7 PINNACLES NATIONAL MONUMENT
Spires, caverns and caves remain from ancient volcanic activity.

Sites of national monuments; areas of historic, scientific or scenic interest.

National Parks

National parks, like the national monuments, are scenic areas set aside and protected by the National Park Service.

1 CHANNEL ISLANDS NATIONAL PARK

Five islands in this offshore preserve—

California's national parks; more areas of outstanding natural beauty.

Anacapa Island, San Miguel Island, Santa Barbara Island, Santa Cruz Island and Santa Rosa Island.

2 KINGS CANYON NATIONAL PARK

Giant sequoias and a huge range of outdoor activities, such as camping, hiking, guided walks and horse riding.

3 LASSEN VOLCANIC NATIONAL PARK

Part of a great lava plateau with interesting remains from ancient volcanic

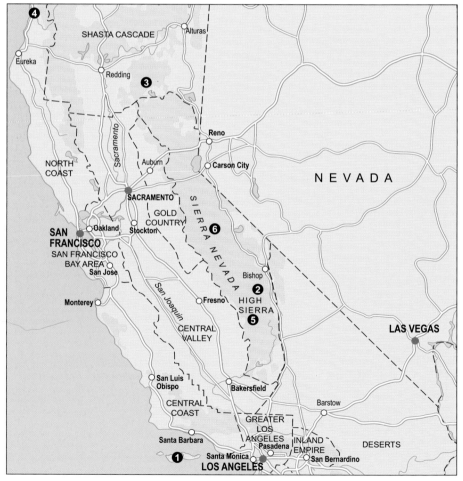

activity. Lassen Peak last erupted in 1914–17.

4 REDWOOD NATIONAL PARK
Includes three state parks lined by Federal land and preserving some of the world's tallest trees.

5 SEQUOIA NATIONAL PARK
Like its neighbour, Kings Canyon, Sequoia offers groves of giant sequoia and summer and winter activities.

6 YOSEMITE NATIONAL PARK
Summer and winter paradise, including beautiful, quiet high country and the very popular Yosemite Valley.

Theme Parks

Theme parks are a West Coast institution, particularly in southern California, and thoroughly enjoyed by the young and the not-so-young.

1 DISNEYLAND
1313 Harbor Blvd, Anaheim.
The number one attraction in southern California.

2 KNOTT'S BERRY FARM 8039
Beach Blvd, Buena Park.
More than 165 different rides and attractions.

3 MONSOON LAGOON WATER PARK
2410 W. Compton Blvd, Redondo Beach.

*T*heme parks for the enjoyment of old and young.

Water theme park ideal for younger members of the family.

4 SIX FLAGS MAGIC MOUNTAIN
26101 Magic Mountain Parkway, Valencia.
Family theme park with over 100 rides, shows and attractions.

5 UNIVERSAL STUDIOS
100 Universal City Plaza, Universal City.
Behind the scenes of the world's largest movie and TV studio.

6 RAGING WATERS
111 Raging Waters Drive, San Dimas.
Water theme park including slides, artificial waves and inner tube rapids.

7 WATERWORLD USA
1600 Exposition Blvd, Sacramento.
Another water theme park with various family amusements.

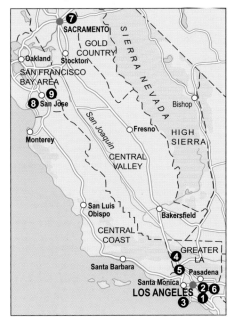

8 GREAT AMERICA
Santa Clara.
Five theme areas taking you through
America's past.

9 RAGING WATERS
2333 S. White Road, San Jose.
Water theme amusement park, including freshwater lagoon.

Television and Movie Studio Tours

Here in the "Movie Capital of the
World", several studios are open to the
public for tours and audience viewing.

1 KABC TV
(Channel 7) 4151, Prospect Avenue,
Hollywood. Tel. (213) 520-1ABC.
Tickets are available for free viewing
weekdays from 9 a.m. to 5 p.m.

**2 NBC TV STUDIO TOUR AND
TICKETS**
3000, W. Alameda Avenue, STE 1501,
Burbank 91523. Tel. (818) 840-3537.
Guests can walk behind the scenes of
this, the only major TV network open
to the public. Free TV show tickets are
also available.

3 PARAMOUNT STUDIOS
860, N. Gower Street, Hollywood
90038. Tel. (213) 956-5575.
Limited public tour of the studios offered, so call in advance. Free tickets
to shows available.

**4 UNIVERSAL STUDIOS
HOLLYWOOD**
100, Universal City Plaza, Universal
City 91608. Tel. (818) 777-3750.
Amusement park cross movie studios,
so put whole day aside. Tram tour and
exciting attractions.

5 WARNER BROS STUDIOS
4000, Warner Blvd, Burbank 91522.
Tel. (818) 954-1951.
Home of Warner Bros and Lorimar
Productions. Personalized VIP tours
are offered (call in advance) and, when
possible, visitors may watch live shoot-
ing.

Winter Sports

Whereas so many people think of California as the sun, sea and beach state,
scattered throughout the state are a
huge variety of winter sporting activities on offer. From Mount Shasta in
the Cascade Range to the Palm
Springs Nordic Center, you can find
anything from small skiing resorts to
Olympic runs, cross-country skiing,

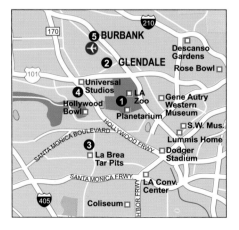

*The television and
movie studios of Los Angeles.*

heli-skiing, snowmobiling, schuss-boomer alleys and ski trails. Contact the US Forest Service in your area for further information.

1 MOUNT BALDY
(off Interstate 10)
A vertical drop of 640 m (2,100 ft) serviced by four double chairs.

2 MOUNTAIN HIGH
(San Gabriel Mountains)
An area of 83 hectares (205 acres) with 90 per cent covered by its own snow-making equipment. A vertical drop of 488 m (1,600 ft), with one quad, three triple and six double chair service. Nearby are Mount Waterman, Snow Crest at Kratka Ridge and Ski Sunrise.

3 BIG BEAR LAKE
(San Bernardino Mountains)
Bear Mountain is the largest in the region, covering 283 hectares (700 acres) and three triple and five double chairs service its 518 m (1,700 ft) vertical drop. Snow Summit covers 85 hectares (210 acres), 95 per cent of which is under a snow-making gun. Other major ski hills include Snow Valley and Snow Forest.

4 MAMMOTH MOUNTAIN
(Southern Sierra Nevada)
Very popular with skiers from the Los Angeles area. Covers 1,215 hectares (3,000 acres), has long season (November–July) and generous amount of ski lifts. Mammoth has also acquired June Mountain to the north.

5 SIERRA SUMMIT
(Southern Central Valley area)
Formally known as China Peak, this is

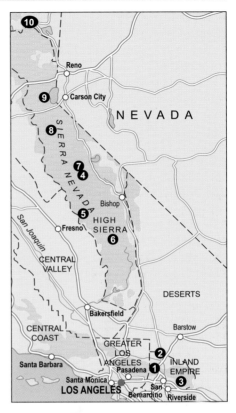

*P*opular destinations for the winter sporting enthusiast.

the only downhill ski area in this part of the Central Valley.

6 SEQUOIA AND KINGS CANYON NATIONAL PARKS
Good cross-country ski areas. Trails and tours. Small downhill ski operation at Wolverton Ski Bowl Sequoia.

7 YOSEMITE NATIONAL PARK
Small downhill ski area at Badger Pass. Excellent cross-country skiing, outdoor ice-skating rink in the valley, snow camping, ski tours and nature snowshoe walks.

8 DODGE RIDGE
(Central Sierra)
Excellent learning slopes and sections
for intermediate and advanced skiers.
Mount Reba/Bear Valley to the north
is medium sized within a beautiful setting.

9 LAKE TAHOE REGION
(North Central Sierra Nevada)
Includes about 15 downhill ski areas
and Nordic centres around the lake.

10 LASSEN VOLCANIC
NATIONAL PARK
Downhill ski area and Nordic trails
through some spectacular scenery.

Scuba-diving

Scuba-diving varies all along the coast
of California. In the south, November
to March is very popular as this is lob-
ster season and the water remains relatively warm. To the north, the summer months are the most popular,
although many like to dive during the
early autumn when the water temperatures have dropped just enough so
that the water quality improves and
the plankton growth slows down. The
following list is a selection of the
better-known sites but for further information contact the local dive shop.

1 LA JOLLA COVE
(La Jolla Underwater Park)
Considered one of the most beautiful
diving spots in California.

2 ORANGE COUNTY
The two most popular spots in this
area are the Marine Life Refuge near

Laguna Beach and the reef off Corona
del Mar.

3 CHANNEL ISLANDS
NATIONAL PARK
A whole range of underwater spectacles can be explored off these islands,
even shipwrecks, but as this is a California State Ecological Preserve, collection is prohibited.

4 MONTEREY PENINSULA
Along the part of the coast south of
Carmel, Break Water Cove (at the
Monterey Yacht Harbor near Cannery
Row) and just off Coral Street in Pacific Grove are the two favourite diving locations of many. Diving can be
done from the beaches or there are
many diving charter companies with
boats available. Point Lobos State
Park is also very popular but can get
very busy.

5 SALT POINT STATE PARK
(NORTH COAST)
Gerstle Cove is excellent for exploring
but is a marine preserve so collecting
is prohibited. Abalone may, however,
be gathered during the spring and autumn.

Whale-watching and Festivals

From December to April, the grey
whales make their long journey along
the West Coast as they migrate from
the Bering Sea to the warm waters of
Baja California and their breeding
grounds. During the summer they
make the trip back with their young.
All along the coast of California,

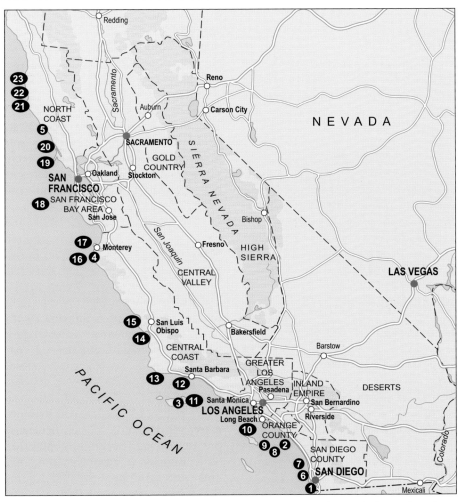

Some of the better places to go scuba-diving (numbers 1–5) and where to watch grey whales (numbers 6–23).

whale-watching cruises operate regularly during the migratory season (reservations are advised) but at several points along the coastland, too, the whales are visible. Specific events surrounding the whale migrations should not be missed. The following list is a brief selection of locations, so for further information, contact: Cabrillo Marine Museum, San Pedro, Tel. (213) 832-4444; Oceanic Society, San Francisco, Tel. (415) 441-1106; Orange County Marine Institute, Dana Point, Tel. (714) 831-3850; Point Reyes Field Seminars, Tel. (415) 663-1200; San Diego Natural History Museum, Tel. (619) 232-3821; Whale Center, Oakland, Tel. (415) 654-6621.

6 POINT LOMA (San Diego)

7 OCEANSIDE
The Oceanside Whale Festival, held during late January, is in celebration of the whales and includes entertainments, arts and crafts, shows and life-size sand sculptures.

8 DANA POINT
The Dana Point Festival of Whales continues for three weekends during late February and early March and includes lectures, films, seminars and special exhibits covering the migration.

9 LAGUNA BEACH

10 LONG BEACH

11 CHANNEL ISLANDS

12 SANTA BARBARA

13 POINT CONCEPTION

14 PISMO BEACH

15 MORRO BAY

16 POINT LOBOS

17 POINT PINOS (MONTEREY)

18 SAN FRANCISCO PENINSULA

19 POINT REYES

20 BODEGO BAY

21 POINT ARENA

22 MENDOCINO HEADLANDS
The Mendocino Whale Festival, held in mid-March, honours the whale's spring migration and includes wine-tasting, whale-watch boat trips, a fish chowder cook-off and tours of the local lighthouse.

23 FORT BRAGG
The Fort Bragg Whaler Beer Fest, held late in March, offers a gem and mineral show, orchid show, beer-tasting and fish chowder cook-off, and helicopter rides to get a different view of the migrating whales.

The Coastal Redwoods

For about 644 km (400 miles) along the north coast of California, from north of San Francisco to the Oregon border, the magnificent coastal redwoods provide spectacular scenery.

1 LEGGETT
A drive-through tree, created by a fire many years ago, is located here in a private grove. The Smith Redwoods State Reserve is located in this area and the 357-hectare (883-acre) Richardson Grove State Park is 18 km (11 miles) to the north.

2 GARBERVILLE
The southern gateway to Humboldt County and location of a year-round Visitors' Center. King Range Wilderness and Sinkyone Wilderness State Park reached from here.

3 PHILLIPSVILLE
From here, exit on to Highway 254 and the scenic bypass known as the Avenue of the Giants. Past some of

the largest groves of ancient sequoias found in the Humboldt Redwoods State Park and ending near Pepperwood.

4 SCOTIA
The largest redwood lumber mill in the world and a lumber town made almost entirely of redwood.

5 FORTUNA
Redwood groves in Rohner Park.

6 ORICK
This is the southern gateway to the Redwood National Park, with 13 km (8 miles) of coastal roads, 161 km (100 miles) of trails and three state parks. Find the Redwood Information Center and from here take a shuttle bus through Tall Trees Grove to see the world's tallest tree.

7 PRAIRIE CREEK REDWOODS STATE PARK
Just north of Orick and thousands of acres of redwood forests with roaming Roosevelt Elk. Lost Man Creek is a short, scenic drive through the redwood forest, though trailers are not advised.

8 KLAMOUTH
Excellent fishing along the Klamouth River and in the freshwater lagoon. Just to the north are the Trees of Mystery and nature trails leading through some beautiful redwoods.

9 DEL NORTE COAST REDWOODS STATE PARK
North of Klamouth with excellent hiking.

10 CRESCENT CITY
The northern gateway to the Redwood National Park and the Redwood National Park Headquarters for all information.

11 HIOUCHI AREA
The Hiouchi Ranger Station is open from spring until autumn and is a good place to start if you are approaching from the east. It offers plenty of information. The Jedediah Smith Redwoods State Park offers excellent scenic drives and hikes through redwood forest.

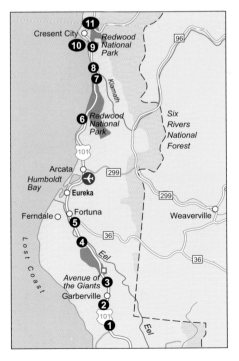

*T*he coastal redwood sites of northern California.

History, Culture, Sea, Sand and Sports in California's Second Largest City

When Juan Rodrigez Cabrillo first anchored off the coast of San Diego in 1542, he might well have thought he had discovered paradise. Today, although it is California's second largest city and one of the fastest growing cities in the United States, it is one of the country's most exciting vacation areas. Despite an immense population growth in recent years, it retains so much of its natural charm and beauty that explorers still find it hard to resist.

Metropolitan San Diego

Most of San Diego's major attractions are located within the metropolitan area, a total of 514 km² (319 square miles). The actual county of San Diego covers 10,360 km² (4,000 square miles), making the city and all it has to offer very accessible.

San Diego International airport (Lindbergh Field) is located just 5 km (3 miles) north-west of downtown San Diego and from here hiring a car is both easy and economical. All the major car-hire companies, such as Avis Rent-A-Car, are located right at the terminal for registration and a frequent free bus service is available to take you directly to your hired car. The choice of transport is huge, including convertibles for those eager to make the most of the warm weather, and maps and any other information you should require are at hand. The roads around San Diego are very simple to get to know. For instance, the main links are Route 5 (or Interstate 5), which runs north to south and is the main road through San Diego, exiting to all the main attractions, such as Marine World, the Zoo and Mission Bay, and Route 8 (or Interstate 8)

All over California, hang-gliding enthusiasts can take to the sky in the peace and quiet of their own company.

59

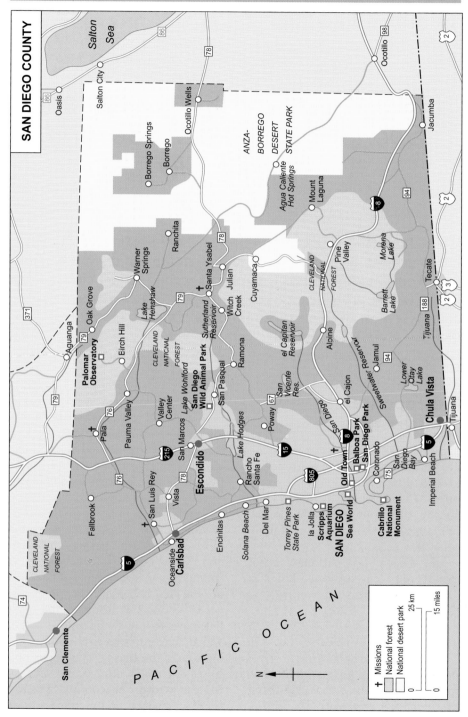

SAN DIEGO COUNTY

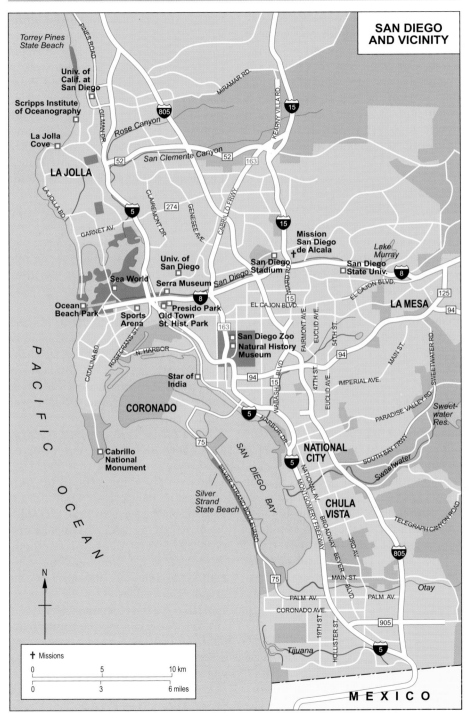

SAN DIEGO
AND VICINITY

Torrey Pines
State Beach

Univ. of
Calif. at
San Diego

Scripps Institute
of Oceanography

La Jolla
Cove

LA JOLLA

PINES ROAD

GILMAN DR.

Rose Canyon

805

San Clemente Canyon

52   52

163

274

LA JOLLA BD.

5

CLAIREMONT DR.

GENESEE AVE.

CABRILLO FRWY.

MIRAMAR RD.

KEARNY VILLA RD.

15

15

Mission
San Diego
de Alcala

Lake
Murray

San Diego
State Univ.

8

GARNET AVE.

Univ. of
San Diego

Sea World

Serra Museum   San Diego

San Diego
Stadium

WARD RD.

EL CAJON BLVD.

LA MESA

125

94

Ocean
Beach Park

Sports
Arena

Presido Park
Old Town
St. Hist. Park

8

EL CAJON BLVD.

15

FAIRMONT AVE.

EUCLID AVE.

54TH ST.

MAIN ST.

SWEETWATER RD.

CATALINA BD.

ROSECRANS ST.

N. HARBOR

163

San Diego Zoo
Natural History
Museum

94

47TH ST.

94

IMPERIAL AVE.

Star of
India

CORONADO

WABASH BLVD.

15

94

5

HARBOR DR.

EUCLID AVE.

PARADISE VALLEY RD.

Sweet-
water
Res.

Cabrillo
National
Monument

75

SAN   DIEGO   BAY

SILVER STRAND BOULEVARD

NATIONAL
CITY

8

5

SOUTH BAY FRWY.

Sweetwater

Silver
Strand
State Beach

NATIONAL AV.

MONTGOMERY FREEWAY

CHULA
VISTA

BROADWAY - BEYER BLVD.

3RD AV.

TELEGRAPH CANYON ROAD

805

N

Otay

75

19TH ST.

HOLLISTER ST.

PALM AV.

PALM AV.

905

5

CORONADO AVE.

MAIN ST.

Tijuana

† Missions

0   5   10 km

0   3   6 miles

M E X I C O

P A C I F I C   O C E A N

61

which runs east to west. Be careful, however, that you don't find yourself in the right lane swept off on to the wrong exit. It is best to keep in the middle lane and give yourself plenty of time to read the exit signs. Anyway, you'll find the speed limit so much slower than in Europe that you won't be rushed into making any hasty decisions.

Taxi and shuttle services and public transportation are available all over the city and tours to all the major attractions are easily located.

Now you're on your way and where better to start than where it all began—the **Cabrillo National Monument** at the southern end of **Point Loma**, named after the Portuguese explorer Juan Rodrigez Cabrillo, who discovered the point on 28 September 1542 and called what he saw San Miguel. Besides being of such tremendous historical significance, from here you can get a spectacular view across Coronada and San Diego. To reach the point, take Rosecrans Street, turn right onto Canon Street and left onto Catalina Boulevard. As you pass through the Naval Ocean System Center, notice the beautiful but eerie **Fort Rosecrans National Cemetery** that lays testimony to the strong military importance of San Diego.

First, stop off at the Visitors' Center located by the Cabrillo Statue

*M*aps showing the San Diego County region (page 60) and the San Diego Metropolitan area (page 61).

where you can pick up all the information you require and see a variety of exhibits, including one on Cabrillo's voyage. From here you can walk a short distance south to the **Old Point Loma Lighthouse**, which, from 1855, served for 36 years (except on foggy nights) as both a harbour light and coastal beacon. It was replaced in 1891 with the more efficient **Coast Guard Lighthouse** still functioning today from the ocean's edge.

There is no better time to visit the park than between late December and the end of February to experience one of nature's great spectacles—the migration of the grey whales—as they pass Point Loma on their 19,300–22,500-km (12,000–14,000-mile) journey from the Arctic Ocean to the warmer waters of the lagoons of Baja California. The best place to see them is at the whale overlook but, for an even closer view, there are a variety of public and private charters to take you out to sea.

Point Loma is also a bird enthusiast's haven, as here, on this westernmost point jutting out from the coast, a huge variety of migratory birds stop off to catch their breath. Don't forget to visit, on the western side, the **Tidepools**, which are rocky environments, protected by law, filled with hundreds of species of marine plants and animals; or to follow the **Bayside Trail**, an insight into the lifestyle of the Digueno Indians who once occupied the Point and on which can still be found remnants of a coastal artillery system that defended San Diego Harbor in the two world wars.

If Point Loma marks the beginning of San Diego, then **Presidio Hill** marks the beginning of California and the home of the first Spanish settlers. It was here, on 16 July 1769, that Father Junipero Serra erected a simple brushwood shelter and established **Mission San Diego de Alcala**, the first of the famous Californian missions. The original mission and the Presidio, which means "fortress" in Spanish, were dedicated to the state's first military settlement, and their historical importance is honoured in the **Serra Museum**, found at the beautifully landscaped **Presidio Park**. Presidio Park is located east of Old Town Historical Park, overlooks Mission Valley, has spectacular views and is an interesting and fun place to take the children.

Today, the **mission church** serves as an active parish for the Catholic community (times of Mass can be obtained from the Parish Center) and a cultural centre for people of all faiths. As it is not primarily a tourist attraction, it is not very well signposted. The **Father Luis Jayme Museum**, named after the padre who died during an Indian attack (*see* panel above) and is buried in the mission sanctuary, is filled with all types of early mission relics. Ask at the Visitors' Center for the Tote-A-Tape Tour.

During the early 19th century, the colonists began to move out of the Presidio and settled in what is now the Old Town, located just below Presidio Park off Route 5 (take the Old Town exit). As the first European settlement in California, up until about 1871 it was the centre of San Diego life. Today the **Old Town** is a state historical park and has been restored and rebuilt in the original style with the help of old photographs. To get a real im-

> **Mission San Diego de Alcala**
> In 1774, the Mission San Diego de Alcala was relocated to its present site, on Mission Gorge Road, 10 km (6 miles) further east up the valley (take Route 8 on to Mission Gorge Road and turn left on to Twain Avenue, which becomes San Diego Mission Road—watch out carefully for signs) in order to be nearer the Indian villages, a reliable source of water and good land for farming. A year later, the timber-dry buildings were attacked and destroyed by Indians and in 1776, the same year as the American War of Independence, reconstruction began on the church and mission buildings, which still look today much as they did then. By 1780, most had been completed and, in 1797, 565 Indians received baptism and the land area had grown to 20,230 hectares (50,000 acres) on which corn, barley, wheat, vines, orchards and vegetables were being cultivated. It is recorded that at this time the mission owned about 20,000 sheep, 10,000 cattle, and 1,250 horses.

pression of early Mexican and American life, first visit the Information Center and take a self-guided walking tour. Or pick up an organized guided tour from the Machada y Silvas Adobe. Within this small area (just six square blocks) you can see where the first American flag was raised, where the first edition of the *San Diego Union* was printed and the old one-room Mason Street schoolhouse. The **Casa de Estudillo**, one of the oldest buildings, dating back to 1830, was once the home of the original commander of the Presidio. The **Whaley House Museum** (1856), the oldest brick structure in the city, now houses antiques and

Old Town was the second dwelling of the early colonists and the first European settlement in the state. Today it is preserved as an historical state park.

period furniture. Also worth visiting is the **Seeley Stables**, filled with stage coaches and other horse-drawn vehicles and western memorabilia (perfect for the children) and **Heritage Park**, on the outskirts of the town, the site of a variety of attractive Victorian homes that have been moved from around the city to this site for preservation.

 But for all the colour, music, food and life of Mexico, it is the **Bazaar del Mundo** you want. Located in the centre of the town on Calhoun Street, this area, once rundown and neglected, has been restored and converted into a colourful melange of top-quality shops and restaurants. For the very

best in Mexican food (and enormous Margueritas to be slowly enjoyed beneath the palm trees while you watch the world go by), visit the **Casa de Bandini** restaurant.

San Diego city centre was to move closer to the ocean again when, in 1857, the entrepreneur Alonz Horton purchased a 15-hectare (38-acre) piece of property and called it New Town. The **Gaslamp Quarter** on Fifth Avenue, once the residence of Wyatt Earp, flourished as the city's first real commercial and business district but then suffered severe decline and neglect, particularly as it played host to the large numbers of sailors on leave who wanted a good time. In 1974, its revitalization and preservation began and today the brick pavements lined with gaslamps and beautifully preserved old buildings lead you through the Victorian era and into a variety of art galleries, restaurants and antique and craft shops. Take a walk along Fifth Avenue to see the **Stingaree**

Building, home of an historic brothel that in its heyday epitomized the decline of this area, and the beautiful architecture of the **Louis Bank of Commerce** building.

Horton Plaza, which is the centrepiece of the "new" downtown and occupies 4½ hectares (11½ acres) between the Gaslamp Quarter and the city's highrises, was named after the enterprising Alonz Horton and was officially opened in 1985. This unique multi-level, open-air entertainment and shopping centre includes 150 speciality shops and restaurants, four large department stores, two performing arts theatres and a seven-screen cinema. Daily entertainment and a variety of cultural exhibits throughout the Plaza gives it a feel of a festive marketplace. If you have any questions, visit the International Visitors' Information Center located at the Plaza.

One of the greatest attractions of San Diego "downtown" living is that everything you need is within walking distance and this really is a pleasant city to walk around. It's clean, friendly and filled with a healthy and youthful vitality. But if you choose not to walk, the **San Diego Trolley Service**, with its bright red trolley cars, is a tourist attraction as well as a reliable way to get around town. The South Line runs from the refurbished Santa Fe Railway Depot downtown to the Mexican border. The East Line runs from downtown to the East County community of El Cajon, and the new Bayside Line is the best service for the Convention Center, city attractions and hotels along the downtown route.

From Horton Plaza, walk out onto the bustling, shimmering waterfront and one of the world's most beautiful, natural harbours. **Seaport Village**, located on 5.7 hectares (14 acres) along the Embarcadero, is a relatively new waterfront dining and shopping centre depicting the harbourside as it was a century ago. If you are a boat enthusiast, the **Maritime Museum**, also located at the Embarcadero, consists of sailing vessels aboard which visitors can relive the days of maritime splendour. Climb aboard the *Star of India*, built in 1863, the oldest merchant sailing vessel afloat; the *Berkeley*, the first successful propeller-driven ferryboat on the West Coast, used in 1906 to carry people to safety during the great earthquake of San Francisco; or the *Medea*, a 1904 steam yacht that served in both world wars.

There is always plenty of action along the waterfront all year round—boats of every shape and size setting sail across the bay; joggers and walkers (don't worry if you see a fire engine or paramedic parked along the way: the drivers are probably out running); musicians and entertainers; numerous world-class sailing competitions; clean, warm beaches and, during the summer months, the San Diego Symphony sets up out by the water to perform.

You may not want to walk the whole length of harbour, 27 km (17 miles) to be precise, but located at the **B Street Pier** is the cruise-ship terminal and an opportunity to see San Diego from the sea. All tickets and information can be obtained at the terminal, where sailing vessels ranging from the *Invader*, an antique schooner built in 1905, to the *Monterey* and *Showboat*, two Mississippi-style paddle-steamers, provide leisurely trips

past the grand navy ships of the San Diego Bay.

The *Silvergate* and the *Cabrillo* carry pedestrians and bicycles frequently throughout the day on a 14-minute journey from the foot of the Broadway Pier to the Old Ferry Landing on Coronado's bayfront. While admiring the view, look out for any sea lions sunning themselves on the floating buoys. The first ferryboat made this journey in 1866, then the most direct and fast link to this island-like community (Coronado is linked by a narrow strip of land, from Imperial Beach to the Coronado peninsula, called the Silver Strand) across the bay from downtown. When the beautiful 3½ km (2.2 mile) arched Coronada Bay Ridge was completed in 1964, water crossing went into decline and was only brought back to life again in 1987.

There is plenty about the San Diego coast that provides the young and the not-so-young with an endless variety of fun and relaxation.

The Old Ferry Landing has been renovated into a quaint speciality shopping area with a perfect view of the San Diego skyline. You can also hire bicycles here, or pick up the frequent trolley, if you wish to venture out and see the rest of Coronado which, although much is occupied by a military base, has some lovely

Bike and jogging paths, walkways and park areas line the coast as the city skyline forms a dominating backdrop.

*T*he world famous Hotel del Coronado has remained an elegant and prestigious hotel since it was built in 1888 (above).

*S*an Diego Mission Park is the largest city-owned aquatic park in the world (below).

residential areas, beaches, boutiques, galleries and restaurants. The world-famous **Hotel del Coronado**, built in 1888, is located on Orange Avenue and is well worth a visit. Still retaining its turn-of-the-century appeal, over the years it has entertained many movie stars, heads of state and presidents and claims to be the first meeting place of the Duke of Windsor and Mrs Wallis Simpson.

Mission Bay, at 1,860 hectares (4,600 acres), is the largest city-owned aquatic park of its kind in the world. It took 20 years of dredging and development and cost nearly $60 million to create this year-round resort playground devoted to boating, fishing, swimming, water-skiing, windsurfing and public recreation. Mission Bay is located just ten minutes from the airport, off Route 5. Any additional information you may require on the park (and other San Diego attractions) can be obtained from the park's Visitor Information Center also off Route 5 at 2688 East Mission Bay Drive.

Access to the 43 km (27 miles) of beaches and parking is free and all the separate sporting activities have controlled designated public areas. There are six public swimming areas with picnicking facilities provided, several marinas, from which one can buy, rent, charter or dock, a full range of watercraft, a water-skiing course, sport-fishing boats for rent and all manner of tackle and bait to hire (a day's catch may be filleted or smoked to take home). Joggers and walkers share the 32 km (20 miles) of running paths near the shoreline and there are also areas within the park to play games such as volleyball or fly all

manner of colourful kites in the waterside breeze. Camping facilities, restaurants and resort hotels, shops and entertainment are easily accessible for those who wish to stay a while.

Perhaps the most famous and popular attraction at Mission Bay is the 55-hectare (135-acre) marine park, **Sea World**. If driving, exit west from Route 5 on to Sea World Drive (all parking is free), or ask at your hotel for bus information. Sea World is an educational treat for adults and children alike and offers a variety of entertaining shows, such as the performing killer whales Shamu and Namu, (sit close to the front if you want to get really wet) and many fascinating

Shamu and Namu, two of Sea World's most popular and enduring attractions.

exhibitions featuring marine life from all around the world. The **Penguin Encounter** is the most comprehensive exhibit of antarctic birds in the world, but other exhibits such as the **Forbidden Reef**, which includes the **Bay Ray Feeding Shallows** (you can even reach out and touch these eerie looking creatures) and the **Moray Eel Caverns**, are not to be missed. If you want to see Sea World and Mission Bay from above, take a trip up 98 m (320 ft) in the **Southwest Airlines Skytower**, which can seat 60 visitors and offers a rotating, 360-degree view; or take a ride on the **Skyride** in enclosed gondola cable cars for a 1-km (½-mile) round trip 30 m (100 ft) above Mission Bay. There are plenty of good eating places and gift shops right here, so make sure you give yourself a full day.

Belmont Park, which occupies 2.8 hectares (7 acres) on the beach at Mission Boulevard and West Mission Bay Drive, is a reconstructed and revitalized beach park whose character as a 1925 amusement park has been preserved. Besides 30 speciality shops, three restaurants, the largest indoor swimming pool west of the Mississippi River, a "high-tech" fitness centre and beautiful landscaping, the park's famous landmark is the recently restored and now fully operational **Giant Dipper Rollercoaster**, which has been created a historical monument.

San Diego is packed full of recreational activities, but for a varied cultural experience visit **Balboa Park**— 435 hectares (1,074 acres) in the heart

At the Penguin Encounter, visitors can drop in and admire a variety of Antarctic birds in an exhibit like no other in the world.

of the city (take the Balboa Park exit off Route 5). Here is San Diego's pride and joy, where one can take a relaxed walk through a variety of beautifully landscaped gardens, past unique architecture, museums, galleries and theatre and outside entertainment that changes all the year round. Balboa Park, named after the Spanish explorer, Vasco Nunez de Balboa, who was the first to sight the Pacific, has a history that began in 1868 when the area was set aside as a city park. It wasn't until 1892, when a private nursery, owned by Kate Sessions, began to operate on park land and paid rent in the form of trees, that the park began to emerge as it is today. Then, in 1915, the first Spanish-style buildings were completed and their doors opened to the Panama-Pacific International Exposition in celebration of the opening of the Panama Canal.

Since then Balboa Park has continued to grow and expand. Anyone interested in air or space must visit the **Aerospace Historical Center**, which is comprised of two museums: the **San Diego Aerospace Museum**, which includes an exact replica of the *Spirit of St Louis*, the airplane that was made in San Diego and took Charles Lindberg on the first solo non-stop flight from New York to Paris in 1927; and the **International Aerospace Hall of Fame**. At the **Reuben H. Fleet Space Theater and Science Center** you can experience all kinds of "space age" and "hands-on" exhibits demonstrating the laws of science. The **San Diego Museum of Man,** a museum of anthropology, houses some of the greatest treasures in the city. Other favourite venues include the **San Diego Natural History Museum**, the **Spanish Village Arts and Crafts Center** and the **Museum of Photographic Arts**. The **Old Globe Theater**, a replica of Shakespeare's own and constructed in 1935 for the California-Pacific International Exposition, was so popular it was made into a permanent structure after the exposition ended. The Old Globe is renowned for the production of world premières of contemporary work. Art lovers should visit the **Timken Art Gallery**, the **San Diego Art Institute** or the **San Diego Museum of Art**. And there is even more to the park, so for further details, including tours, maps and opening times, visit the Information Center.

The world-famous **San Diego Zoo**, in Balboa Park (Route 5 south, past Mission Bay) is not only the city's leading visitor attraction but also the largest and most innovative zoo in the world. Forty hectares (100 acres) in an ideal climate means that around 4,000 animals of 800 species can be exhibited outdoors, year round, in unfenced, moated enclosures which resemble the animal's natural habitat. The easiest way to see the huge animal population is to take the 40-minute guided tour, which covers about 70 per cent of the zoo, through miles of winding roads down canyons and up the mesas. A variety of endangered species, such as the pigmy hippopotamus, and animals seldom seen in zoos, such as the long-billed kiwis from New Zealand and the wild Przewalski horses from Mongolia, have their home here, not to mention the largest collection of wild birds in the world. Exciting exhibits include **Tiger River**, a trek down a mist-shrouded path to explore the wonders of an Asian tropical rain forest

The Sumatran tiger, a feature of the Tiger River exhibit, is just one of the many unusual and rare animals to be encountered at San Diego Zoo.

(including Sumatran tigers, Malayan tapirs and web-footed fishing cats), and the new **Sun Bear Forest**, where among giant trees, tall grasses, streams and waterfalls, rare lion-tailed macaques and frolicking Malayan sun bears live. The zoo is open daily from 9 a.m., and an information booth is located at the Camera Den, left of the main entrance, for times and details of all the attractions.

If you are planning to stay in San Diego a while, a day trip to Tijuana, Mexico is a must. **Tijuana** is the most visited border city in the world and, with the decline of the peso and Tijuana's status as a free port, it is a shopper's paradise. Its bazaar-like atmosphere attracts bargaining from even the most shy, for a whole variety of Mexican goods such as leather items, jewellry, pottery, glassware and clothing. There are three ways of making the journey to the border. The easiest is probably with local tour operators (check through your hotel or any Visitors' Information Center) or the relatively new high-speed trolley service that runs from downtown San Diego. If you decide to drive, Route 5 south takes you right to the border (*see* pages 9–10 for customs and passport requirements, limits on purchase and suggested insurance).

If you decide to drive to the international border (or even if you don't but would like a good day's shopping), stop off at the **San Diego Factory Outlet Center** in San Ysidro at exit Camino de la Plaza, the "last US exit". Here you'll find a huge selection of shops selling top-named brands at discount prices.

La Jolla

Travelling north just 15 minutes from downtown San Diego, just beyond the popular beach community of Pacific Beach, set along 11 km (7 miles) of rugged coastline, slightly secluded and surrounded by rolling hills, is the resort town of **La Jolla**. Indeed a polished diamond set among the jagged shards of uncut crystal, La Jolla (pronounced "La Hoya" and meaning "the jewel" in Spanish) combines the charm of a quiet Mediterranean island with top-class hotels, superb restaurants, excellent shopping, magnificent scenery and an endless array of leisure activities.

For the centre of La Jolla shopping and dining (and make sure you give yourself plenty of time to browse), head for the palm-tree lined **Prospect Street**, which is filled with all the colour, energy and youth of the area. Parking along the street is strictly limited to one hour, so park in the underground car park located midway along the street just to be safe. Fine boutiques, art galleries, jewellry and clothes shops, bars and restaurants line the street, enclosed in quaint outdoor arcades that stretch out above the waterfront. From the back of some of these shops you can get a wonderful view of the ocean. If you are feeling energetic, from the back of La Jolla Cave and Shell Shop there is access to the seven caves, at the southern end of the **Ecological Reserve**, part of the famous La Jolla Underwater Park. The 133-step descent (and corresponding ascent) is well worth it. The steps wind through a tunnel into the largest of the seven caves, colourfully named Sunny Jim.

The **La Jolla Underwater Park**, which extends from the southern boundary of the University of California San Diego to Goldfish Point near La Jolla Cove, is filled with a variety of beautifully coloured fish and interesting ocean formations and is a favourite place for scuba- and skin-divers. The Ecological Reserve, a strictly "look-but-don't-touch" area, was established in order to preserve the natural beauty of La Jolla Canyon and to protect its underwater treasures of flora and fauna.

The rugged coastline of La Jolla is a water-lover's paradise. La Jolla Cove (follow Coast Boulevard from Prospect

The Californian coast offers superb underwater experiences and photographic opportunities.